GREENVILLE COLLEC

Richard W. Bock Sculpture Collect

Memoirs of an American Artist —sculptor, Richard W. Bock

edited by
Dorathi Bock Pierre

is being sent
to you through
a generous gift
from
John C. Herklotz
to
Greenville College

Greenville College is a four year, liberal arts educational institution located in central Illinois, about one hour east of St. Louis, Missouri. Through its Department of Art, degrees are offered in art and art education with specializations in painting, sculpture, drawing, ceramics, art history and graphic design.

The college's enthusiastic support for humanities education, especially in the realm of the fine arts, inspired the heirs of Richard W. Bock to donate over four hundred sculptural objects plus thousands of photographs and documents for the establishment of the Richard W. Bock Museum on the campus in Greenville, Illinois. The museum has hence become the primary cultural asset of central and southern Illinois, providing access to the rich historical and aesthetic tradition in which Richard Bock worked. The collection also serves as an important resource for those interested in the Prairie Style and its architects, being the largest and most comprehensive display of any single artist associated with the Prairie School of Architecture.

John C. Herklotz, from the Middle West, a graduate of De Paul University, was financial officer for seventeen years with the Chicago Tribune/WGN Broadcasting. Moving to the West Coast, his business interests in broadcasting and communications as president of Cellular Financial Corporation, led him to the entertainment field and especially family entertainment in films, which he is now producing.

Additional copies
of this book may be
purchased from the
Department of Art,
Greenville College,
Greenville, Illinois
62246
(618) 664-1840

His contributions have been wide in scope, from medical, including Alzheimer's research, to the restoration of an historical church in Santa Fe, to music scholarships.

He early became aware of the value of the arts in education and the need to encourage them. Expanding his gifts, he made donations to Greenville College for the specific purpose of distributing the memoirs of the well-known sculptor, Richard W. Bock, lovingly edited by his daughter, Dorathi Bock Pierre.

It is the hope of Mr. Herklotz and of Greenville College that *Memoirs of An American Artist—sculptor, Richard W. Bock* will be of interest to you and may encourage arts education and a greater support of art in public places.

315 East College • Greenville, Illinois • 62246

Memoirs of an American Artist
Sculptor

RICHARD W. BOCK

Edited by

Dorathi Bock Pierre

Library of Congress Catalog Card Number 89-90127
Copyright © 1989 by Dorathi Bock Pierre. All rights reserved.
Published by C.C. Publishing Co., Los Angeles, California
Second Printing 1991

To the memory of my beautiful mother

MARTHA METHVEN BOCK

Father's inspiration and loving companion

*To laugh often and love much; to win the respect of
intelligent persons and the affection of children; to earn the
approbation of honest critics and to endure the betrayal of
false friends; to appreciate beauty; to find the best in others;
to give of one's self; to leave the world a bit better, whether
by a healthy child, a garden patch, or a redeemed social
condition; to know that even one life has breathed easier
because you have lived — this is to have succeeded.*

Ralph Waldo Emerson

Contents

Introduction

My father, the sculptor Richard W. Bock, was born in the small West Prussian town of Schloppe on July 16, 1865. Little is known of his family background, except his parents were both German; his father's family descended from 12th Century Teutonic Knights, and his mother's family "were professors, teachers, postmasters, and an explorer who went to Australia in 1870."

When he was four years old, his parents with their three small children, Richard, an older brother William and a younger sister Marie, emigrated to the United States to join relatives in Chicago, Illinois.

His father, Frederick William Bock, was an artist wood-carver, cabinet-maker who worked on many of the ornate wood carvings for Chicago's mansions and churches.

In due time he took out citizenship papers which also naturalized the minor children. Father was always proud of being an American, and when he prepared to spend several years in Europe as a student, he took out his own papers so there would be no doubt of his citizenship.

When father was in his early seventies he became aware of a lessening in muscular strength, and as he had always been a strong and active man he was disturbed and sought medical help. At that time doctors did not diagnose his ailment and treated him with massage and diet. The condition did not improve and eventually was diagnosed as Parkinson's Disease. In the late thirties there was very little known about the treatment for this disorder.

Father's greatest enjoyment had always been his work, and he found restriction of his activities very difficult. Always a good story-teller and a facile writer, he embarked upon a double project: the completion of an exhaustive work on Sculpture Techniques, and an autobiography, both of which he had started sometime before. He continued these projects under increasing difficulty until his death.

In 1972 my brother, the artist Thor Methven Bock and I, gave the extensive collected works of our father with other art works and memorabilia to Greenville College in Greenville, Illinois, to establish the Richard W. Bock Museum which was dedicated in 1975.

Dr. Donald P. Hallmark, curator of the collection at that time, assembled the autobiographical materials, put them in order and had typed copies bound for the Museum Library. Dr. Hallmark also authored two exhaustive books on the sculptor's works.

I have taken father's free-flowing autobiography and edited it for this book of memoris which offers a view of one man's life as an artist.

Dorathi Bock Pierre
Sherman Oaks, California

Chapter I
1870-1879

I was four years old when I left Germany with my parents to come to America in May, 1870.[1] There were my parents, my older brother William, younger sister Marie, and a baby who died.

We came on a sailing ship, and I remember very little of the distressingly uncomfortable journey which took, nine weeks. I remember a small area of the deck and the area below deck which seemed always crowded, where there was no privacy.

I was later told how the ship nearly capsized several times in terrible storms, but there were also calms that lasted for days when not a sail would stir and the people thought the ship would never land.

I remember one day when I saw some of the sailors carrying a large board with something tied on it. They rested it upon the ship's railing; everyone was gathered around the place, and someone said something and I saw a man sobbing. Then the board and what was tied on it fell into the water. After that everyone was very quiet and the crowd soon dispersed.

I remember nothing of landing.

My first memory of America was riding on a train and stopping at a place surrounded by hills they called Pittsburgh. It was a lovely spring day and my father got off the train to buy some food. He brought back some bread, coffee and milk, and almost missed the train.

We arrived in Chicago the year before the great Chicago fire. Living quarters were soon found and furnished. Father found work as a cabinet-maker, and my brother William, who was two years older than I, was sent to a Lutheran perochial school near by. I envied him when I saw that he was the proud possessor of a slate and slate pencil, and a book with pictures to copy. I decided then that I wanted to make pictures like those. When the family budget permitted purchase of another slate and pencil it was the beginning of my art career. I was very happy and delighted with my humble efforts. After my pictures were adequately admired by my mother who was a kind and loving parent, I wiped off the drawing to give way for another demonstration of my skill. Finally, my father became sufficiently interested to buy me some paper and a lead pencil and some real drawings to copy. Then my drawings could be saved and I was able to see what progress I had made. Sometimes visitors gave me some pennies if I made a special drawing for them.

One of my greatest pleasures was to sit in front of a black walnut bureau we had and admire the carved wooden drawer handles representing a pear with leaves at each side. I wished one day to be able to do that kind of carving. Childhood seemed awfully slow before I could be a real artist.

When at last I reached the age of six I, too, went to parochial school. Of course I studied history and georgraphy and the three "Rs." But what interested me most were the fascinating stories of the Bible. They stimulated my imagination beyond anything else. It was all real to me, all of my emotions were stirred to the utmost, just as they were by the fairy stories I read and which I still enjoy. I believe they stretched my imagination and meant a great deal to my development as an artist.

I did not spend all of my time drawing or studying. I loved to play, and was involved in everything. Life was one adventure after another. I will refrain from relating details of two near drownings.

I impatiently awaited the time of graduation from school. The teacher in the advanced term was a mean and cruel man who practiced corporal punishment for the slightest reason. Several times his hated rawhide whip disappeared in spite of threats of dire retribution. He had a number of children of his own; the oldest was in my class, a frail girl of thirteen, who beside attending school, often had to stay home to help her mother with the other children. Then, when she did come to class, not knowing her lessons, he would take this poor helpless victim and beat her with that wicked rawhide. I wished then I were grown so I could protect her. I remember well that hard feelingless face and I could draw it today line for line. He had a habit of holding his hand with the palm up and pointing his long boney finger in a reverse arch. I drew it on the margin of my book and he saw it but only made a moderate remark about it.

To get out of singing lessons I pretended to have no ability to sing, so to save his ensemble he excused me. One time he sneaked up on me playing his fiddle and he gave me a sharp whack on the head with the bow, breaking it. I expected a beating, but nothing happened. For some reason I never really drew his anger, and he put me at the head of the class. He probably wanted to be sure to get rid of me.

Graduation and Confirmation both came at Easter when the pupils received special training in the teachings of the Lutheran religion, both at school and Sunday school, with examinations which were finally concluded by the ritual of the Holy Communion.

For this important event the children were fitted out with new clothes, and although it was a holiday it was an agony from which we wanted to escape. After the graduation services my brother and I went for a walk, and it was not long before we were out of the city and in a prairie. It was spring, the ditches were full of water, and far beyond were men hunting. My brother had already become interested in hunting and he wanted to go nearer. We started toward them, trying to catch plovers that kept leading us on just out of reach. Finally we were in a field of mud and pools of water with no trace of dry ground. We forgot the hunters and trudged along in desperation with an occassional plover flying overhead screaming at us, but we were no longer interested in catching birds.

In fear of the consequences of our truancy we started home, arriving just at dusk. Our parents were anxiously waiting for us but said nothing, and I will never understand how we avoided punishment.

This was the last incident of my childhood, and also the end of my student days for some time. This was the year 1879 and in a few months I would be fourteen years old and entering the road to manhood with all its challenges.

At no time during these early years had I ever neglected my precious drawing, and up to this time I had never had a lesson in drawing, or a criticism.

Chapter II
1879-1884

In spite of my interest in drawing I decided I wanted to be a sculptor. Over vehement remonstrances on my part my father had made up his mind that I must first have security and get a job as a cabinet-maker as he had done, so for the time being I had to surrender to his will. I put in two years assisting him working in a furniture factory.

One of my first duties was to get small pails of beer for the men's lunch, carrying about six or eight on two notched sticks. I did not have far to go, for in those days there was a saloon on every corner. My compensation for this service was a free lunch sandwich or a nickle or dime once in a while. I learned how to sweep the floor and keep the fire burning for the glue pots. I also learned how to use a wood plane properly, and to use sandpaper until my fingers bled. Most important, I learned work discipline.

There was a depression at this time and restlessness among the workers. I have always been sympathetic to the labor movement because skilled workers like my father and myself, working together ten hours a day at piecework, were unable to make more than nine dollars a week. The security and benefits labor has today were unknown then.

The heads of great industries were daring, hardworking pioneers. They were capable, venturesome men who felt they had earned every cent of their gain, and intended to keep it for themselves. This was and has always been the sentiment of those who have succeeded, and still remains a bone of contention with labor. Workers at this time were attempting to unionize under the name "Knights of labor."

On the fringe of the labor movement was a radical group made up of socialists, communists and anarchists. Twelfth Street Turner Hall in Chicago was a favorite meeting place where they voiced their grievances and demanded action. The small group of radical agitators with their doctrine of force was an obstacle to the growing strength of the labor movement. They published several newspapers and called numerous meetings that frequently ended in fights and bloody confrontations, ending with the historic Haymarket Square Riot in 1886 when a number of people were killed and many injured and arrested. It is remembered as a "world rocking tragedy" but resulted in sweeping changes for the betterment of labor and the world in which we live.

Many years after the fateful Haymarket Riot I was called upon by a confessedly reformed anarchist. He had with him a design for a tablet commemorating that fateful event. I executed the model of that design; it is in bronze and is incorporated in the Haymarket monument in Waltheim cemetery in Chicago.

I still worked at my job and clung to my dream of being a sculptor. There were a number of wood-carvers where I worked and I watched them and asked questions of the foreman who was a very good carver. He was an elderly man with a very long beard, fully three feet long, which he tucked inside his vest. His name was Schrumpf.[2] I had been buying carving tools, one at a time from my small allowance, and using them in my spare time. Finally I asked to be a carver. Everyone seemed to favor my request, even the boss was agreeable, but it was Mr. Schrumpf's interest that won the opportunity for me. He made a wager with the boss that in three weeks I would be able to carve an eagle with spread wings, the most difficult piece of work they had in the shop. Now I had to buy more of the tools I needed and I did not have the money. My intelligent and loving mother helped persuade my father to buy me the necessary wood-carving tools, and I was put at a woodcarver's bench. The bench was high, coming just under my elbow, and the tools were laid out with the cutting edge toward me. By the nature of carving, the carver's head is bent sharply forward looking down upon the work. At the end of the first day I had a very painful stiff neck, but I was at last embarked upon my career as a sculptor.

I made good on all that was expected of me, and Mr. Schrumpf won his wager with the boss. By the end of three months I was earning seven dollars a week; that was big wages then. Mr. Schrumpf also secured a scholarship for me at the Mechanic's Institute of Chicago. I attended night classes three nights a week, taking free-hand and mechanical drawing, geometry and English grammar. At the same time I was keeping up my drawing at home with the help of Mr. Schrumpf's criticism.

About this time I heard of a sculptor, a Mr. Almenraeder, who gave Sunday morning classes in modeling. I added this to my curriculum and worked with him for two years. My health and stamina must have been excellent to have carried such a load.

I also became aware of feminine charms. Sometimes on my way home from work I would stop and look into a certain stationary store window where they displayed the Police News and Police Gazette showing buxom females, large of hip and dressed in tights. I acquired several sweethearts at a distance. One thrilled me greatly, a Helen-of-Troy type of beauty. She was the daughter of the hardware dealer where I bought my carving tools. I remember how happy it made me every time I caught a glimpse of her and how sad the days I did not see her. Fortunately for me she knew nothing of my infatuation for one day I saw her pushing a buggy with a small infant in it, and I felt somehow jilted. I could not go on with that love any longer so I found another. This one was vivacious, full of life, and all the boys were chasing her. She belonged to my brother and sister's crowd, and I had spoken to her once. I knew where she lived, and I would go out of my way to pass her house and wait, hoping to see or meet her. I never did have the courage to ask if I might call on her, and I gave up my vigil upon learning the object of my secret devotion was engaged to someone else.

I never joined in the social activities of my brother and sister and their friends. I had too much work to do to fritter my time in such activities, and I knew my time for amusement would come later. However, I did love the theater, and whenever I had spare time and some change

I went to a performance. The atmosphere of the theater was intoxicating. I saw most of the great players of the day. I remember especially Edwin Booth, George Barrett, John McCullough, Edmund Kean, Joseph Jefferson, James O'Neill, Mary Anderson, Julia Marlow, John Drew, Ada Rehan and many more. I prefered to spend my time with them in the world of make-believe.[3]

I had not been carving a year but there was no more for me to learn where I was working. There was comparatively little variety in the character of the work in any of the shops, and very little of any art merit; speed was the main objective. A fellow carver and I were put to work on the same design in order to ascertain the time it would take to complete the job. My fellow carver and I were close friends and he was especially good and twice my age. I was eighteen and very fast, so I timed myself so I would not finish before him. As a result, my friend kept his job and I found myself without one.

I had become very proficient in modeling and plaster casting through my Sunday morning lessons, so I soon got work with an interior decorating firm. This was far more interesting than the work I had done before. I was on my own and had no foreman over me. Mr. A. Grossman, my employer, and a few of his artist friends got up a life-drawing class which I was permitted to attend. This was a most unusual experience for me at my age. It was a thrill in more ways than one when I saw a nude woman for the first time. I was greatly disturbed by this revelation, but in future classes sex did not again overwhelm me.

There were slack periods in the interior decorating business but I had no difficulty finding another job immediately; this time with my modeling teacher, Mr. Almenraeder. He asked me to carve a life-sized horse. The main requirement being that it fit a furnished harness. After that I felt perfectly competent when asked to carve a wooden Indian, the kind that stood in front of cigar stores. Carving these large effigies was an invaluable part of my early training.

Once, while working along side a man we got into a discussion of the meaning of charity. Thinking to score a point for Christianity I asked him what he would call a fellow like the one in the story of the Good Samaritan who gave away all he had to the needy? Unhesitatingly he replied he would call that man a damn fool. So I got another shock, but I was growing up. I began reading Thomas Payne's The Age of Reason and The Rights of Man. I was deeply impressed by Robert Ingersol, Huxley, Spencer, Darwin and Voltaire.

About this time I joined a society of free thinkers called "The Liberal League of America." It often occured to me while attending their meetings that this liberal society was capable of narrow intolerance, and though I was very moved by liberal ideals I always managed to keep an objective balance.

Unfortunately my interest in progressive thought brought me into strong conflict with my father, with the result that I left home.

Chapter III
1885-1887

A friend who had recently returned from New York assured me that there was nothing more for me to learn in Chicago, that New York was the best place for me.

At the time I was learning a new technique at the North Western Terra Cotta Company where they were just starting to use terra cotta as a building material. I had asked for a pay increase which did not come through so I went to the foreman, and on impulse told him I was going to New York. He was surprised but went to the superintendent who offered me a good increase in salary to stay. I refused it and told him my reason for going to New York was to study and improve myself as an artist. He approved my objective, said he admired me for it and wished me well.

In three days I was on my way to New York. I was determined that nothing would stand in the way to learn more about my art. I had one difficult farewell, I had at last entered into a real love affair. To my sensitive nature it was a very serious matter and we had a touching parting, which was the last time I ever saw her. Though we corresponded for some time, the flame flickered and finally went out.

The approach to New York along the Hudson River and the Palisades, with a golden sun shining through a mist on the water is unforgettable. We passed fishing villages one after another, just awakening, with some early fishermen already out in their boats. The imposing grandeur of the Army's West Point high on a hill is inspiring. On and on thundered the train to deliver me into the arms of the waiting metropolis, which did not know or care that I was coming like thousands of other young hopefuls, with the determination of making a mark for myself.

Arriving at Grand Central Station, I checked my grip and had something to eat. I soon found a room around 27th and 8th Avenue where I had an unexpected view from my window. Across the yard, plainly visable through an open window was a view of provocative female nudity that was my welcome to the temptations of New York. After a good night's rest I was ready for job hunting, but it was not until the third day that I found one, with the great Herter brothers, the outstanding interior decorators and furnishers.

I soon joined the Union so that when there was no more work at Herter's another job was waiting for me with Allen and Ketson, the leading architectural sculptors of New York. They were then doing the architectural decorating, woodcarving, plaster and stonework for the Vanderbilt mansion on Fifth Avenue. The work being done was in the style of the Italian Renaissance after Sansovino. I have never seen that style reproduced with better feeling, and I enjoyed working on it.

I had to overcome a lot of prejudice from the other men because I was from Chicago. Because they were New Yorkers they felt superior. With spare time during the lunch hour the men went around the shop inspecting the work being done. I was interested in the modeling shop, and spoke to Karl Bird, the man in charge. I told him of my experience and learned they were looking for a modeler and were willing to give me a trial. They had already tried several modelers who could not do the work.

As I began gathering up my tools to transfer to the modeling shop I heard many jibes, as "The kid carver from Chicago thinks he is a modeler. He'll be only too glad to be back with us again." And, as I passed Mr. Blum the foreman, he smiled and wished me good luck. He and the others did not know that the work to be done was not new to me and was easy and fun to do. I was amused the following day when the men came around inspecting my work to see them speechless. It was a little triumph for me.

Karl Bird soon made a proposal that we share a room together which turned out to be very satisfactory. He had recently come to America from Germany and he wanted to Americanize himself very quickly. We were lucky to find something to our liking on 27th Street between 6th and 7th Avenues.

Mrs. Cynthia Leonard and her family also lived there. Mrs. Leonard was a very attractive-looking woman, seventy years old, six feet tall, stately and erect with fine-cut features. She had five daughters, all blond, and they worshiped their mother. Among them was the beautiful actress, Lillian Russell. Hattie Leonard, the oldest and only one unmarried, lived with her mother. The Leonards and I became very good friends and Karl Bird and I remained friends through life. I lived there as long as my work lasted, which was about a year.

Mrs. Leonard was a remarkable woman who practiced dumb-bell exercises every morning. She donated her time and money to social betterment, contributing a library to the city among other things. She was interested in a Free Thought society, and I would often escort her to evening meetings where she would lecture and take part in debates. While walking to these meetings she often urged me to make plans to go to Europe to study, and I decided to take her advice.

When there was no more work for me at the shop I made plans to return to Chicago to prepare for my sojourn and studies in Europe. It was hard to say good-bye to the Leonards and Karl Bird, but the encouraging words of Mr. McLain, the superintendent of Allen and Ketson, pleased and encouraged me.

Back in Chicago, and after a week's rest, I found myself at work again with Mr. Almenraeder, my first modeling teacher, carving a number of heads in oak wood. They had hardly been completed when the building caught fire destroying all but a large front corner room on the second floor which I used as a studio. The room was flooded with water but the fire never touched it. My work and all one hundred and twenty-five of my carving tools were safe.

I soon began work again at the Terra Cotta company, and found they were looking for a foreman. I hurried to tell my friend Almanraeder and he was hired and proved to be the right man for them. I stayed there nearly a year, working and saving money. The following year I planned to leave for Europe with enough money to see me through at least three years of study.

I had many art books on ornament and other design subjects, and a lot of plaster casts which would not be of future use to me. I could not sell any of them for a satisfactory price so I arranged a raffle to dispose of them. This netted me much more than I had expected, and I am sure the generous prices were a friendly gesture on the part of my friends for a good cause.

Chapter IV
1888-1890

My intention was to be in Berlin for the fall enrollment at art school there. With my papers in order, ship and railroad tickets purchased, I was once more on my way to New York where I had allowed enough time to see my friends and say good-bye.

I had a strange and almost disastrous experience the day my ship sailed. I had taken a room during the day before at a small hotel near the docks of the German Lloyd Line in Hoboken. I left word with the clerk the time I wanted to be called in the morning, and paid in advance. I then went into New York, saw my friends and went to a party with Miss Leonard. I got back to the hotel well after midnight, went to my room and was surprised to find the door unlocked, but I was very tired, just undressed and dropped into bed. I awoke with a start to find the sun brightly shining through the venetian blinds. I looked at my watch and saw I had twenty minutes to get to the ship. In three minutes, partly dressed, I was down at the desk. The clerk hailed me, wondering where I had been. When I had not answered his call he had brought down my belongings including a bag of oranges he had found in the room which were not mine. It seems I had slept in the room next to mine. I grabbed my things including the fruit, tore out of the place and down the street, collar and tie hanging out of my pocket, vest unbuttoned, unwashed, uncombed, overburdened, and oranges dropping along the way.

It was like a comedy. I was almost there and the band was playing as if to accompany my one last effort to win the race of my life. I was alongside the ship when the guards saw me and beckoned me on. The passengers on the ship were waving handkerchiefs and shouting good-byes to their friends on the dock, but it was as if they, too, were cheering me on. I reached the gangplank, and in a last mighty effort, with the help of the guards, I was hauled aboard the ship.

My ocean trip this time was pleasant all the way, but just commonplace: good food, smooth sailing, no seasickness, no drama, no comedy, only restful and lovely, even beautiful at the sight of a merchant ship passing within speaking distance in the moonlight.

Best of all, we arrived at Bremerhaven in less than nine days where a train for Berlin was waiting. My first impression of the countryside through which we passed seemed a very dark green, drab and rather depressing.

An uncle, who lived in Berlin had been expecting me, and I stayed with him for a few days. He seemed bored after our first walk to orient me, and I saw that he would be of little help and that I would have to attend to my own affairs. Fortunately I spoke German.

The next day I went out alone, walking along Unter den Linden where there were art galleries and art stores. A small sign alongside a passageway leading into a court caught my eye. It read "Max Unger, Karten und Vinettern." At last I would see an artist. I went in and met a very pleasant and obliging young fellow whose advice was helpful. I then went to the Kaiserliche Konigliche Kunstgewerbe Museum where I was to study, and matriculated.

The following day I would decide what courses I would take. I would also find lodging near the school. My uncle was impressed by what I had done and acknowledged that Americans worked fast.

I was determined to get all the benefits offered to a young art-hungry American student. With all of the preliminaries completed, classes started and my student life in Germany began.

My studies took all of my time, six days a week, leaving only enough time for eating and sleeping. Modeling was my major course. Three hours in the morning, three hours in the afternoon and then four hours each evening covered life modeling, life drawing, anatomy and architecture. The instructors were all excellent and I advanced very rapidly.

About the middle of the term a competition in composition was given with a first prize of eighty marks. The subject was a lamp post. After the models were judged, the coveted slip of paper with "First" on it was found attached to my model.

Not long after this pleasant surprise another occured. There was a class custom to model an appropriate trophy for the professor's birthday. Anyone could offer sketches, and mine was unanimously approved, and I executed it.

The night before his birthday the piece was taken into Professor Behrendt's private studio. When he came to class the next morning he was generous in his appreciation of our birthday gift. He was usually a taciturn fellow but now he rose to the occassion. He invited the whole class, about fourteen of us, to a party that evening in a private room at a popular tavern. He had arranged for a sumptuous dinner and we made merry with glasses of beer and student songs.

Our professor was in a happy mood, and when he wheedled out of someone that I had made the design of the trophy, he shook my hand, thanked me and praised me further. He said he would have it photographed and give each of us a copy. Professor Behrendt was a good scout and a fine teacher, but he sometimes lost patience with the noise we made during our heated arguments.

I wanted to take some classes at the Academie der Bildenden Kunste, but it was difficult without considerable pull. I did have a good contact through a student in my day class, Ludwig Vordermeier. He was the nephew of the celebrated sculptor, Mathias Vordermeier, who was then executing a piece of marble for another sculptor, named Kafsack. I decided I would like to work with Kafsack so I could work in marble, and offered my services as a volunteer. It was arranged for me to enter his studio, and I found the work I wanted, carving three large marble keystone heads of Minerva, Juno and Mars for the public library in Leipzig. He paid me so I did not have to work for nothing. Also employed by him was a sculptor from Vienna named Rudolph Schwartz, a clever fellow with whom I soon shared a room.

Sculptor Kafsack had a very amusing temper when something went wrong. At one time his plaster caster returned the plaster cast of one of his models which had a blemished surface, saying the gelatin mould got mulmy. Kafsack flew into a rage. "Mulmy is it? Mulmy!" He leaped over chairs and boxes, striking his head with his hands and shouting "Himmel, Herr Gott, Sacrament, Sacrament, Sacrament! Is that what I am paying money for? Himmel, Herr Gott," over and over until exhausted. Finally it was over; he was calm, affable and smiling as though nothing had happened.

One of the first conversations I had with my uncle on my arrival was about an artist scandal that was making front page news. The stars of the drama were a model, a perfect nude named Bertha Rother, the artist Jaeger and the complaintant wife. The cause was the painting "Das Maerchen," a portrait of a beautiful female emerging from a fish skin. It was a fine painting, well done. Now the beautiful model Bertha was causing gossip by emerging in sculptor Kafsack's studio.

It was customary at the beginning of the school year to elect a new board of officers for the school fraternity consisting of a president, vice-president, treasurer, secretary and their assistants. The Germans call this their Auschus. The result of our election gave me the greatest number of votes for the office of treasurer. Being a member of this Auschus is held as quite an exalted honor, for it seemed to be formed as much for show as for service to the students. The officers of the organization had a distinctive regalia consisting of a velvet beret with a gold rope suspended in front, and a red and white sash worn over a cutaway coat. At outdoor functions the group's standard was carried on display. This standard was of exceptional beauty and craftsmanship, and was very heavy, weighing over fifty pounds. Because of my six foot height and strength, I was always delegated to carry it with the help of four others who steadied it with ropes.

On the whole we were a congenial group and we often had lunch together. We were a gossipy, jovial crowd. Once they decided I had an inordinate appetite for bread, and two or three continued baiting me about it when we got back to the studio. I took it good-naturedly thinking they would get tired and stop, but they kept it up to the amusement of the entire class. Standing near me was a young Alsatian who was being egged on by the bully of the class. I finally tired of this and told him to stop. Instead he turned to make another taunting remark saying "He. . ." but he ended up lying on the floor. I went back to my work but the bully was not satisfied. A big hulk of a fellow, he came at me in an aggressive attitude and I got into position to take him on. He thought better of it and retreated with lofty words about honor, decency, violence, a blot on the school, and that I should be expelled for fighting. I was never bothered again, and the Alsatian, really a good chap, became one of my best friends.

I enjoyed my work at the school very much, especially the night classes, and I was decidedly good in all of them. In those days anatomy was the basic principle of sculpture. Professor Maxmilian Schaefer had us take dictation from his discourse each session, and because of my lack of speed in German, he permitted me to copy from his manuscript after class which was a decided advantage.

We had to draw every bone of the entire skeleton separately and we had to draw carefully where and how each muscle was attached to the bone. It was splendid training in drawing and I enjoyed it. The muscles were drawn from large colored charts on paper the size of the drawing board. For elucidation the professor took out from a cabinet sections of an embalmed human cadaver wrapped in linen, smelling of carbolic acid and resembling smoked meat. Professor Schaefer loved anatomy, and so did I. I enjoy remembering him. He was a talented, charming man and a fine teacher. His textbooks on anatomy, printed in English, have been extensively used in this country.

There was a fine library where I studied and sketched in my spare time. I would get up at six o'clock in the morning, go to the zoological gardens before visitors arrived and sketch animals.

It takes a special technique to draw the restless, moving beasts. You settle upon a certain action of the animal you want to sketch, watch it intently, concentrating upon it for several minutes in order to have a likeness of the animal and its movement in your mind; then quickly draw from the picture in your memory, being careful not to disturb the image by extraneous objects around you or intrusive thoughts. You are as it were, in a kind of trance. I would look at a lion striding for about ten minutes, then I would go outside the building, sit on the grass, and draw from memory. To do this well takes practice and the concentration of a trained artist. I made a series of sketches of lions, and a one-third life-size picture of a panther and other animals. I especially enjoyed doing this, and found it very relaxing.

Christmas was always a lonely time with thoughts of home. One Christmas eve, my friend Ludwig Vordermeier and I were sitting in his room, feeling sorry for ourselves, in a state of desperation for something to do. Finally he said "I feel like doing something unusual," and he proposed that we go for a hike through the Grunewald Wood about ten miles outside Berlin by train. I was unable to think of anything more foolish so we went. It was about eight o'clock and we had had our dinner so we were ready to leave at once. Passing along the street and seeing lighted Christmas trees in the windows did not add comfort to our prevailing mood. We reached the station just in time to take the train to our strange destinatioin. As we got off the train the conductor eyed us with suspicion for no one else got off, and it was a dark, desolate place.

There was not a house or light in sight, and the ground was covered with several inches of snow. We struck a path leading into the woods and walked until we came to a barbed-wire fence. So simple an obstacle could not stop such intrepid explorers. I ripped my trousers getting through only to find myself on the very edge of a high bank of a flowing river. That decided us we had had enough; our appetite for adventure was sated, unless we found more trying to find our way back in the dark. We were willing to substitute the imaginary thrill for the real as we thought back to ancient times when giant elk and bears freely roamed these woods.

New Year's eve we fared better. Ludwig and I were invited by his uncle, sculptor Mathias Vordermeier, to the celebrated Pshor-Brau. This uncle, a very handsome man with a black beard trimmed like a Hofmann

Christus, was not only a fine sculptor but was one of Germany's finest yodlers. He was Bavarian and they, like the Swiss, are born yodlers. As the evening advanced the patrons became more jovial. An organ-grinder came in grinding out some tune upon which our host raised his silver bell-like voice and rippled out the loveliest, most entrancing yodeling I had ever heard. When he stopped there was wild applause. Getting up, he took the organ-grinder's hat and went to a number of tables taking up a collection which he gave to the man. The applause continued until he again gave full measure of his beautiful voice.

At least once a year there were gatherings at the school called Commers, to reaffirm the fraternal pledge of the student body. Three or four hundred students sit at long parallel rows of tables. The officers in full regalia sit at the middle table, the president at one end, the vice-president at the other. Both have swords with which they rap for order. Ladies are the honored guests and sit in the balcony. The first toast is drunk to them. "Ein Salamander furden Frauen" and everyone raises his mug of beer. Then "Rub the Salamander" is shouted and all the mugs are rubbed on the table followed by three taps. A good swallow of beer is taken after which all the voices are raised in "Lang soln sie leben, lang soln sie leben, drie mal hock." The mugs are drained, the empty mugs are banged down on the table and all sit down. Everyone is toasted: the school, the faculty, the Vaterland and art. Then the "buddy" toasts are made when, with arms linked, they toast each other with much merriment and banging of mugs. Everyone has a good time; it perpetuates the student spirit and relieves the tedium of study.

Once again I had the delightful experience of being in love. She was a Jewish girl I met at a gathering. She was the most bewitchingly beautiful woman I had ever seen. I was invited to her home for dinner and met her family. They were fine people and well to do. she gave me every reason to feel encouraged, and I invited her to the artist's costume ball. The theme of the ball was the orient, and I went as an Arab. Among the decorations was an Arab tent where we could lounge unseen. Another Arab and I put on an act with spears and shields. We staged a fight that must have been good for we were applauded until we gave another demonstration of our prowess.

After the ball, the parents called for their daughter in a carriage, and I was invited to call again, a pleasure I gladly accepted.

I realized I would have to make a decision: to follow the course of love, which would have been easy, or the more difficult one of my dedication to art. It was a question of "to be or not to be" totally devoted to art. After the mental turmoil was over art prevailed, and I wrote my darling an emotional letter explaining why I could not call.

My plans for admission to the Academie der Bildenden Kunste had brought favorable results thanks to the friendly intercession on my behalf, and I was very pleased when I was told I could register for the 1889 fall term, and added these classes to those at the Kaiserliche Schule.

I am sorry to say that the school was a great disappointment to me. Housed in dilapidated quarters, the instructors did not instill enthusiasm in our efforts. The head professor came only once or twice during the entire year to criticise our work. The assistant professor, Janensk, was there every day but he was a colorless individual and did not inspire anyone.

There were only eight students in my class. One of them, named Hundrieser, son of a prominent sculptor, was proud of his strength and took on anyone who would wrestle with him. This would-be champion was young, strong and short, and had already thrown several when they urged me to try. Much against my will I agreed. I had seen what his method was; he maneuvered around for an opening for an underhold which I could not prevent because of his size, but I would not let his head bore into my chest. I guarded against this by having both hands in a ready position to grasp his head whereby I had a perfect leverage on his neck because of my height. I kept my legs far apart and firm, grabbed his head and pressed it back enough to hurt, then with a sudden jerk I unbalanced him. He kept turning, trying to break my hold. He doggedly held on, whirling faster while I exerted more pressure on his neck until he finally let go his hold and rolled into a corner. After that he never again challenged anyone to wrestle with him. Beyond this I can say no more about him or the Academie.

Berlin in the summer time was a drowsy, lonesome place after the school closed and the students left for home. I was the one who could not go home. My friend Ludwig went back to Munich. I decided to go to Potsdam to do some sketching. That is where the Royal family spent their summers. It is the equivalent of Versailles in France. It was laid out by Frederick the Great who favored everything French. He called his chateau Sans Souci — without care. I spent most of the summer there, delightfully, and to good advantage.

There is a large quantity of fine marble sculpture from several periods in the extensive garden grounds. Of special distinction are those by the French sculptor, Gaspar Adam. I sketched everything I saw.

After four happy weeks I returned to Berlin and called upon my uncle. He, his wife and fifteen year old son were just preparing to go to the so-called Saxonian Swiss Alps for a two week vacation, and they invited me to join them. I was very glad to accept but insisted that I would take care of my own expenses. The scenery was indescribably beautiful. We stopped at a mountain resort opposite a government fortress with a moat and drawbridge dating from medieval times. It interested me so I took out my sketchbook and started to draw. A guard was walking back and forth, and upon seeing me sketching he came up to me and said that such things were not allowed. I explained that I was a student at the K.K.K. Gewerbe Museum School and the Academy of B.K. both in Berlin, and I was only doing an art study. While we were talking I kept right on drawing. He came up to me several more times before I was through. He all but implored me to stop. Pointing to the officer's quarters in the inside court yard, he explained that if they saw us, as they very easily could, it would be the dungeon for him. When I saw my uncle and told him of my experience, showing him the sketch, he almost fainted. He held a high government position, and he explained what the awful consequences might have resulted from my sketching, picturing both of us being dragged away in chains. The name of this fortress was

Koenigstein, and it was where the Kaiser's treasures were kept. It took some time for my poor uncle to recover from the shock.

Back in Berlin I still had several more weeks before school opened again. Part of the time I spent making a portrait bust of my uncle and the rest in visiting the museums and libraries.

School opened and I took the same courses as before, a routine of diligent hard work, but there were the fraternity rites and other incidents to relieve the routine.

One of them was a visit to Berlin by Buffalo Bill and his Wild West Show. Annie Oakley was there with her wonderful sharp-shooting. Bill Cody was a very picturesque man, and a good actor. There were Indians and cowboys, Indian ponies and even some cattle. The German public was so impressed that they believed Indians and cowboys with their six-shooters still roamed the streets of big cities in the United States.

About this time, the sculptor Kafsack, a yachting enthusiast with his own yacht, invited two friends, a painter and an architect to go for a sail. They were caught in a sudden squall and the yacht sank with the architect the only survivor. The officers of our school fraternity participated in the funeral services which were held at the grave. Many noted artists came to pay their last respects to the great sculptor. Standing conspicuously alone, dressed and heavily veiled all in black, stood the only woman mourner, the model Bertha Rother.

I began making plans for a year of study in Paris. Many of the German students in my classes longed to study in Paris, but they knew that since the War of 1870 they were persona non grata in France. My room-mate Rudolph Schwartz, who had worked on a model for a Kaiser Wilhelm I monument for the university city of Halle had received the commission to carve it in the native rock on the Salle River in Saxony, and was devoting all of his time to it. It would mean a great deal to his career and he was jubilant when I saw him off at the train. Unfortunately it was the last important work he did before his untimely death.

This left me with only one real friend, my pal Ludwig Vodermeier. Talking one day to his landlady, I told her of my plans to study in Paris. She said she had a brother living in Paris who would be glad to help me get settled. He spoke German and English as well as French. She promised to give me a letter of introduction to him and to inform him when I would arrive.

My second year of study in Berlin was uneventful. I had covered all of the subjects and all I had to do was apply myself with constant industry and concentration to perfecting my work, in which I made good progress.

During the following spring vacation a group of about fifteen of us went on a long hike in the country to an ancient cloister ruin near the village of Corien, near a lovely small lake framed with large old oak trees. As the sun was setting we gathered at a local inn. After good food and drink the singing began and continued far into the night. The good villagers were being robbed of their sleep, so the mayor who was angry, ordered the lone night watchman to stop the din at once. When the watchman appeared in the door we were spellbound and for a moment speechless. He looked like a story-book gnome. He was not over five feet tall and his overcoat which was much too big for him reached almost to the floor. He wore a great belt and suspended from a heavy cord around his shoulder was a horn made from a goat's horn through which he could blow an alarm. He had on the funniest shaped hat above a comical kind of old face. He carried a stunning old lantern and a halberd. Ludwig was the first to recover and advanced with open arms, welcoming him as one of our own. Others offered him glasses of beer which he first refused and then accepted. He was a rare sight, like figures to be seen in the paintings by old Gothic masters. Our revelry soon came to an end and we slept on sleeping pads the inn keeper had laid on the floor for us.

Ludwig and I and some of the others were up early to enjoy the sunrise. The cloister ruins were not too interesting. Only four solid brick walls remained of what had been a huge four story Gothic building, the kind the Tutonic Knights erected after their return from the Crusades.

It was a beautiful day and passed pleasantly until we met at an agreed time at the village restaurant and dance hall. It was early and the band instruments stood idle, a challenge to us to take possession. One of the boys who played the piano well struck up a Strauss waltz just as several waitresses came in to take our orders, and they immediately fell into the arms of the rest of us who whirled them around the floor. Again, the good citizens of Corien appealed to their Burgermeister to get rid of "diese wilden Berliner studenten." But the happy studenten having completed their dinner, soon formed a "gaenesmarsch" single file like geese, and with a lusty "Auf Wiedersehn" were on our way. When we came to the outskirts of the village we were joined, unbelievably, by a flock of young geese which persisted in following us to the great distress of a young boy and girl who were tending them. The little girl was in tears and the mother goose was sissing at everybody. Our rear marchers finally had to stop and chase them back.

The time I spent in Berlin was during a period of Germany's greatest prosperity. Everyone was happy and it seemed like a perpetual holiday.

My two years at the Kaiserliche Konigliche Kunstgewerke Schule and Museum were drawing to a close. I had learned a great deal and I was grateful to all of our instructors. As a mark of appreciation I modeled a four-foot statue representing genius holding a skull upon which he is placing a wreath. At its base I put the words "To our Professor." He was really moved and thanked me profusely.

By the last semester I had completed all the arrangements for my departure for Paris. My sojourn in Germany with its excellent training had been profitable, and I was grateful for the many privileges granted me as a foreigner.

As I write these memoirs there are daily reports of massive bombing of Berlin. I am saddened, and pray my beloved alma mater may be spared.

Before I left I wanted to pay a visit to the place where I was born. It had the unromatic came of Schloppe, and boasted of being called a town though it had only three hundred inhabitants. In a small way it was a rather picturesque place. I had some relatives living there, but I did not know them and felt no connection to the place so, after a few days I returned to Berlin. But I knew it would please my mother that I had paid my respects.

Chapter V
1890-1891

Ready to leave Berlin, I called upon Ludwig's landlady for the letter of introduction to her brother in Paris.

My final act in Berlin was to go to the Cook's Tours Agency to arrange my travel route, procure my tickets and the indispensable Baedecker guide with its red cover. My route to Paris was from Berlin via Leipzig, Halle, Frankfort, Wiesbaden by train, and then by way of the Rhine to Ruedisheim and Coblenz where I would disembark and take the train to Frier, Mets and Paris. I arranged layovers in places that were of special interest to me. For reason of convenience and economy I travelled with very little luggage.

Leipzig was my first stop. I wanted to see the three large keystones which I had carved in marble in Kafsack's studio, and were now over the doors of the new library building.[4] The city had many cultural interests and architectural monuments. In Germany it ranks next to Berlin as a city of great importance in size and beauty. I stayed there for a day and did some sketching. Some time later Leipzig erected the most stupendous soldier's monument in the world, designed by the architect Bruno Schmitz and the sculptor Karl Metzner.[5]

Halle had a large university that was a center for liberal and radical thought. Through my friend Rudolph Schwartz I was able to visit a well-known student's meeting place where their "Mensuhr," which was a fencing event, was held. The participants wore a partial mask over their face and head, and some other body protection. It was a matter of great pride to have a conspicuous saber scar about the head or face. . . I knew a fellow who kept his head shaved in order to display a large gash on the top of his head. These scars were considered marks of manhood and were cherished decorations. What was an unforgettable sight for me was the extent that the hall, some forty by eighty feet in size, had been splattered with blood, the ceiling as well as the walls. It was revolting, but it was a rare privilege to get into the place, as the students considered it their "sanctum sanctorum."

From Halle I went to Frankfort, stopping there for some hours, long enough to see the town, the Cathedral and the Goethe House, home of one of Germany's intellectual giants.

My next stop was Wiesbaden, a famous health resort with curative waters. From there I took a steamer on the picturesque trip down the Rhine, where every hill is covered with the celebrated grapes that make the famous Rhine wines. All along the winding course of the river the landscape is dotted with castles that are hoary with age and legend. There are some in the middle of the river, rearing aloft their fanciful architectural forms where they have braved the rushing waters for hundreds of years.

I stopped at Ruedisheim which had one of the largest wineries in

Europe, famous for its splendid wines. My object in stopping here was to see a very famous monument a few miles beyond. It is a thirty-two foot high bronze statue representing Germania, called the Niederwald Denkmal. As a work of art it is of no consequence, just an advertisement for a departed monarchy. I stayed there overnight as it was late afternoon when I arrived. I walked around the town but it soon became dusk so I went to an inn called Die Kindenwerthin where I got something to eat and arranged for lodging. I sat on a bench at a long plain board table in a dimly lighted room. There were only a few local burghers in the place who conversed on local matters as they smoked typical German pipes and drank beer from colorful steins. It was a scene with the characteristics of a painting by Kraus. It was a dreamy kind of place with an old atmosphere and I had some of the Ruedisheimer wine in a glass which held fully a pint. Not being much of a wine drinker I soon felt its effect so I settled my dinner bill and was directed to my room two flights up which I had to climb. How I ever got there remains a mystery, for when I awoke next morning I found myself lying across the bed fully clothed. But for all that, I felt no aftereffects and did recall the wine tasted very good.

After a hearty breakfast I looked forward to another pleasant day. I started by viewing the Denkmal Monument, and then I had lunch at a Weinstube that had an interesting rich interior and furnishings. I took a seat at a heavily carved oak table covered with a fine lace cloth. The chairs were particularly interesting, having backs heavily carved in high relief of various imaginative figures. I ordered wine which was served in an exquisite glass I accidently broke and had to pay for. The town also had an interesting villa dating from the time of the Roman occupation by Emperor Trajan in the year 101 A.D.

I was soon on my way again, down the Rhine, passing the beautiful "Burg Pfalz" and the mysterious "Mause Thrum" in the middle of the river. Then, all of a sudden, after turning a bend in the river, there rose out of the water the majestic, massive rock almost a thousand feet high, known as "Der Lorelei Pfelsen." Heinrich Heine made it famous with his "Song of the Lorelei." At sight of this majestic rock the passengers spontaneously burst into song, making the Lorelei Rock truly memorable. On and on we went, through a panorama of beautiful scenery.

Far down the river stood an odd stone structure representing a flight of steps rising to a large flat platform. It is simple and massive, and is called "Der Kaiser Stuhl." Upon that platform Charlemange was crowned Emperor. On this journey I had seen the most beautiful scenery of the Rhine River.

At Coblenz I left the boat. This city was the site of a great fortress, called Ehrenbreistein, a Gibralter-like rock which once was considered impregnable, but today it is only a scenic landmark. From here I took the train for Paris.

We entered France by way of Metz. We passed Lyon Belfort, scene of a disastrous Napoleonic battle, marked by a wounded lion done in bronze by Frederic Bartholdi, who also designed the Statue of Liberty which stands in New York harbor.

On reaching Paris I checked my luggage and went to find the

landlady's brother, Neo Hirsch. This was easily accomplished with the aid of the most polite and obliging Parisian police. He and his wife and daughter were expecting me and they greeted me warmly and made me feel immediately welcome. Everything had been arranged. I would live with a Spanish family in the same building, who could speak English, and I would have my meals with the Hirsch's where they spoke both German and English.

I did nothing the first day beyond getting acquainted and making plans for things that had to be done immediately. The following day Mr. Hirsch took me first to the Bureau of Registration with my passport, then to the American consul to get a letter of recommendation permitting me to study at the Ecole de Beaux Arts. Our next destination was the school where I found the director, Paul de Bois, a most obliging gentleman who gave me the choice of working in Cavalier's or Fulguire's studio. I chose Fulguire's class. I do not remember the tuition fee, but there was a studio contingency fee of 80 francs, paid to the appointed head man in the class. With fifteen or more students enrolled, it made quite a nice class fund.

After getting my luggage at the railway station we went home and called it a day. I became intimately acquainted with the Hirsch family during my year's stay in Paris, and I remember them fondly.

When I went to the Ecole de Beaux Arts I found everything in readiness for the first session. We all made the payment to the class fund, then each student took a modeling-stand, armature for a three-foot figure, and some modeling clay from a large box where it was kept damp. On a revolving stand was a nude male model, and after a number of suggestions a pose was chosen. After these preliminaries a recess was called and everyone was invited to go to a nearby cafe for something to eat to be paid for by the student fund. I was the only one of the six American students in the class who joined these little gatherings. I wanted to get acquainted with the life of my classmates, and to learn the language. There was a Swiss student named Sigwardt, an intelligent fellow who spoke German and English as well as French. He was somewhat older than I and he often offered me valuable advice. He did well in his career, and years later in the United States I came across illustrations of some of his work.

Practically all of the American students in the class that year became capable, outstanding sculptors. There were Bella Pratt, Hermon MacNeil, John Flannagan, a fellow by the name of Pike and another from Ohio who returned to Ohio and became an art teacher. We were six out of a total of fifteen students, a high percentage of Americans.

The highest performance in life modeling at the Academy was by an American sculptor, Frederick MacMonies. A cast of one of his works stood on a shelf as an honor and an inspiration to us all. For our first life class we had the same model that had posed for MacMonies' statue.

It was worth noting the keen competitiveness and self-confidence of everyone, for we all had years of preparatory training. We would appraise each other's effort and exchange friendly criticism during the model's rest periods. We labored industriously, but nothing sensational resulted.

There was one fellow who had a wonderfully discerning eye and a clever technique that enabled him to put up a very striking figure for the first few days. But it did not improve the longer he worked at it, showing that a facile technique alone is not enough without a basic knowledge of anatomy.

We American students were never able to put our modeling stands in the best places near the model, it was the outer rim for us. John Flannagan, having other classes, would often be late and find no preferred place, and after working awhile under such difficulty, he would become exasperated, break up what he had done and leave the class, muttering a few choice American cusses as he went. On the other hand, modest, quiet Bella Pratt, a hard worker, seemed satisfied to be off in a corner where the light was poor, almost behind the model, a place no one wanted. Left rather alone, he concentrated his whole attention on his work. Though it seemed uninspired and cold, his work had a rich, articulate surface. It was of pronounced merit, but no one liked it. However, proving how mistaken we all were, at the end of that subject when the studio award was made, to the surprise and bewilderment of all, the little piece of paper with the coveted words "The First" written on it was found on Pratt's model.

When professor Falguire came to class and was asked why, he pointed to the model on the stand "There is your problem, look. You were to render a likeness of that model." And he could have added "I did not want you to give me a demonstration of just any figure." It was quite obvious then that there was no better work than Pratt's for he had made an exact likeness and we had all tried to show how clever we were. Today his work ranks with the very finest. A pity his career was all too short.

After spending two weeks on our first project we were ready to change to another model, this time a female, a young Italian girl. She had posed for one of Falguire's celebrated marble statues of Diana that was copied and eagerly purchased by American collectors. She was of a stocky type with small joints, hands and feet. For study posing in class, a simple easy-to-hold pose was always selected, so no artistic or interpretive idea entered into the modeling. When the professor came in the morning the students thought it would be interesting and instructive to have him pose the model as he had her pose for his statue. It was a remarkable demonstration, as he moved each limb, the body and head into a position of animation. Now the figure was that of the goddess of the hunt; beautiful, graceful and alert. A revelation that inspired all of us.

There was a young chap in the class, a nephew of the professor who was a pest to everyone. His favorite amusement was to throw pellets of clay. While absorbed in our work, a pellet would suddenly strike one in the face. This had happened to me several times when I decided I would give him a surprise. I went quietly up behind him, took him in my arms, and with him struggling, dropped him into the big box of soft clay. The French students all shouted their approval and hailed me as a brave American. They probably had been inhibited by his relationship to the professor. The young man gave up his pellet throwing after that.

The French students were a capable and industrious lot. It was apparent they were all striving to emulate the style evolved by their great master sculptors from the French Revolution and Napoleonic periods.

It was Caesarian or Empire, which can be translated into Greco-Roman Classic in art, architecture and pageantry and glamour. In this style Louis David, the painter, was the outstanding genius, and he devoted himself with fanatic zeal and enthusiasm to the glorificatioin of that new order of "Liberty, Fraternity, Equality."

An event of greatest importance toward the modern movement in art was taking place with the return to a stern classic form. These were stirring and serious times, and art that had been created to please the few now was making way for the expression of art for the many.

The new expression of modern art grew splendidly, thanks to a number of much earlier pioneers, notably Pierre Bontemps, Germain Pilon and Jean Goujon, all of the 16th Century. Goujon's fountain "Des Innocents" with its charming bas relief of nymphs draped and spaced in most exquisite fashion, his carytids, and the large marble group of Diana with deer that is in the Louvre, are modern for all time, and classic art as well. All students of sculpture have at some time slaked their thirst for fine bas relief sculpture at Goujon's fountain. It is an extraordinary example of this most difficult sculpture technique.

There seems to be no doubt that two sculptors of the early 19th Century influenced the art of their time: Albert Thorwaldson, a Dane, and the Italian Antonio Canova. They had quite a vogue, but the classic revival seems to have been spontaneous as it manifested itself in everything related to art. Instead of the cold classic form, however, the French turned to a more life-like expression, the wonderful outpouring of talent of Rodin, Muenier, Bourdel, Dalou and Berias, Debois, Mercier Chapu, Fremiet, Pusch, Paul Auba, Delaplanche, Gerome, Coutan, Bartholome, Injalbert and more.

A. L. Barye proved himself a great sculptor in the special field he had chosen; he devoted himself exclusively to modeling animals, an area in which he achieved greater and more lasting fame than any other French sculptor. Not generally known is the fact that he spent a large part of his creative years in the city of Baltimore, through the generosity of that city's foremost art patron, William T. Walters.

The French government had a grandiose plan for buildings and parks programs to beautify the city of Paris. It created an enormous demand for master sculptors, painters and innumerable craftsmen. All strove toward the same goal with the same inspiration: to keep alive the tradition of France as the world center for art and culture.

The government in its wisdom, has always encouraged and supported art in every form, and in turn art has been its best commercial and national asset. France has more art than all the rest of Europe put together, with the exception, perhaps, of Italy.

The first Academy of Fine Arts, the Ecole de Beaux Arts, was founded by Mazarin in 1643, and the Academy of Architecture by Colbert in 1671. Both of these schools were amalgamated during the Revolution in 1861 as the Ecole de Beaux Arts. It was by far the finest school in the world in which to study art.

The school had a fine library and museum, and I made full use of both. I was particularly impressed by the display of copies of practically all of Michelangelo's works, including his Sistine Chapel ceiling, painted by Prix de Rome students, showing the energy, drama and spirit of that great master of the Rennaissance.

The class in anatomy was presided over by Professor Duval. He simplified anatomy and made it interesting. He demonstrated its mechanism by the overlaying muscles in relation to their points of contact over joints, resulting in the most interesting patterns of angular designs in both human and animal figures. This knowledge helped me later in creating some uniquely stylistic pieces of statuary and effective architectural decorations.

Since a little relaxation is always desirable we had a party paid for by the student fund. I went with my friend Sigwart, and was the only American in the group of about eight or ten. We went to a restaurant popular with the students where good food was served to those with lean purses, and where refinement of dress was not required, where freedom of thought and conduct was part of the menu. Everyone was happy, and to continue this mood, a visit to Bal Bullier was suggested and met unanimous consent. This place of amusement was a large hall frequented by students of the Latin Quarter, where they carried on in gay abandon with plenty of doubtful ladies eager to assist them. You had to be a native to participate in the frolic for it was not only risque from the point of view of sex, but plain risky for safety. When our group got there they dove right into the mass of gyrating, shouting, singing humanity on the crowded floor. A number of girls were riding pick-a-back atop men's shoulders. Indescribable antics were going on. My pal Sigwart and I sat safely at one side of the hall, considering ourselves well compensated as spectators only.

I had changed my living quarters from my good friends, the Hirsch's to an old hotel called The London near the Beaux Arts on the Rue Bonaparte. In spite of its shortcomings it was very convenient, only a few minutes from the studio. This change of location gave me two or more hours a day to devote to my studies. I kept up my associatioin with the Hirsches and went to see them every Sunday. I was regarded as one of the family, and it seemed like home to me. I was very fond of them and grateful for their kindness. Neo Hirsch was a Jew, born in Germany, his wife was a Parisian and Catholic, and their seventeen year old daughter was Lutheran, born in Berlin.

There is an interesting story about this lovely young girl named Jeanette. Mr. and Mrs. Hirsch had lived in Berlin and had a small store of some kind in a tenament district, a neighborhood that always harbors a promiscuous assortment of characters and breeds children that spill over into the street. At evening time the youngsters scurried for their homes except one little girl who stayed behind even when it got dark. She would stand by the lighted window of the Hirsch's store and finally would just sit down and go to sleep there if the police did not take her home to a mother who did not love or want her. Most of the time the Hirsches took care of her, and they became very fond of the child and wished she was theirs. Finally they brought it to the authorities and it was agreed by all to allow Mr. and Mrs. Hirsch to adopt the child legally. A really happy ending for the little girl.

Mr. Hirsch's business in Paris was that of an agent for small imported items which took him all over the city. As many of my afternoons were free from classes, he would arrange his time so I could accompany him and see new and interesting areas of the city. There were parks, plazas, monuments and architectural gems everywhere.

One time one of these trips took us to the city walls. It was late afternoon and already bats were flying through the air getting their evening meal. This added to the atmosphere when we came to a very old peasant-style cottage with a small fenced-in garden. "We will go in here. I think you will be surprised" said my friend, and he whispered further "She is a Spiritualist Medium." The lady was pleased when I was introduced as an artist, and she immediately became very animated, pointing to some pen drawings on large sheets of paper pinned to the wall. She claimed she had done them all while in a trance and that she did not know how to either read or write, and never had a lesson in drawing. The idea of art coming from a mind unrelated to it was startling. As far as her art was concerned I would place the madam as an early pioneer in modern surrealist expression.

The Hirsches lived next door to a furniture store called Crepin et Dufaelle, located on the corner of the Boulevards Magenta and Barbes. It was owned and operated by Madam Dufaelle who was about sixty years old and the head and soul of the place. She held monthly Sunday afternoon concerts in a huge ballroom in the building. The musicians were all musically trained employees and everyone was welcome to the free concerts. The ballroom was in the style of the Paris Opera with a gallery and large crystal chandeliers. There was a wall fountain and two beautiful twenty-foot high tile paintings on the wall designed by Galland. There were also full-grown potted palm trees. The concerts were always crowded, and the employees enthusiastic in praise of the madam.

Of equal interest to the ballroom was another very large room at the rear of the building, long and high-ceilinged, where about thirty magnificent horses who pulled the delivery wagons were housed. It was airy and light, finished completely in glazed tile. All of the trim and fixtures were polished brass. It was immaculately clean and orderly, a true showplace reminding one of the famous royal stables in Vienna.

That building was only a short distance from the great Church of the Sacre Coeur, which stands on the highest part of Montmarte and has a splendid view of the city. The building stones of the church, in the Romanesque style of architecture, were each paid for by an individual and inscribed with the donor's name.

Not many blocks down from the church was the notorious Moulin Rouge dance hall. In earlier days it was called Moulin la Galette. On the street at the rear corner of the building there was a well, about thirty inches in diameter and three feet high. It had long ceased to function as a source of water. It was discovered that a new use had been found for the well when the outrageous occurrences in the dance hall led to a brutal murder and the investigation for the missing body led to examination of the bottom of the well. What was discovered was a gruesome revelation: the skeletons of four males, two females and a small infant. The old building was immediately torn down and the well destroyed. Sometime later a new Moulin Rouge was erected on the site.

Our small group of American students were an industrious lot. Not content with only morning classes, we arranged to have our own extra afternoon class in one of the student's studios and to have the American artist, Frederick MacMonies criticise us. His fine knowledge and experience were of great value to us.

Occasionally we took an entire afternoon off, went to a park and played the good old fashioned American game of baseball, which was the only time we had any real exercise except for walking. Actually I did a great deal of walking, there was so much to see, and I was eager to see everything. I loved Paris.

I had a visit from my friend Karl Boil from New York, who was on his way to Germany and had stopped off for four days to see Paris. I put him up in my room. My friend was of short and stocky build, and he did not like to walk. I stressed the point that to see Paris one had to walk. Just to walk across the place de la Concorde, without stopping to look at any of the numerous sculptural works of art, would take over ten minutes, and to the right and left and beyond everywhere the sculptural masterpieces one must walk to see. The Louvre, greatest art museum in the world with its countless galleries and art treasures, only to walk through without looking at anything, would take two hours.

After two days of sightseeing my friend was so tired and disgruntled that I had to find a professional guide who could, he thought, arrange things so there would be less walking. They first went to Fontainebleau, well worth seeing at any effort. It is about forty miles from Paris, reached by electric railway. At Fontainebleau, the distance from the station to the palace is one and a half miles. He used a taxi and all other points were reached the same way so his walking was much reduced. I would walk and take a week to see it all: the forest, the Barbizon where the great Millet lived and painted. Also Corot, Breton and many other of the immortal French artists. The next day my friend planned to see Versailles. It is about ten miles from Paris. It, too, took a whole day, but not nearly enough to see so much. The fountains alone are a great work of art. Then there is the great palace with its Hall of Mirrors where so often the human comedy has been played out. After my friend got home that day he was not only weary, but tired of what his guide was costing him. That admission was comforting to me, and I had the pleasure of loaning him some money.

But there is so much more to see. There is the Pantheon in which the remains of the great immortals are interred, with fine marble portrait busts and statues of those entombed there. The walls are covered with huge paintings of historic subjects by a number of France's finest painters. At the entrance to this magnificent building is Rodin's celebrated statue "The Thinker." It was here that the physicist, Jean Bernard Foucault, suspended a pendulum from the center cupola 350 feet high, to prove the earth's rotation.

Another temple-like building in a beautiful, spacious setting is the Dome des Invalides, which contains the tomb of Napoleon; a hugh polished sarcophagus, resting upon a large, plain block of dark polished granite. In a circle surrounding it are a number of caryatid-like female figures ten feet tall, holding wreaths. With the sunlight streaming through stained glass windows into the hazy light of the sombre interior, it truly impresses one as a holy of holies. That all of this grandeur was for the repose of the Emperor Napoleon I, makes one pause to consider the greatness and also the smallness of man.

Often, when I could get up early enough, I would go to the Jardin des Plants. Here are the wild animals, botanical gardens and the Ethnological Museum where the human spicies is represented, oddities and all, in plaster models, many modeled from life. One of them was a Hottentot woman and child that Malvina Hoffman, the American sculptress, took exception to as it was admittedly repugnant. Sometime later she modeled her version of the same subject for the hall of Man in the Field Museum in Chicago.

Wherever I went I took my sketch pad with me and always did a lot of sketching, which was of enormous benefit to me.

I often reflect upon the many beautiful parks of the city, all containing beautiful works of art. Park Morceau is notable for a large oval Corinthian colonnade partly standing in a lake, which is an artistically created ruin with some of the columns fallen and broken, and parts of the cornice down. It is further enhanced by very effective planting. Surrounding it are numerous statues and monuments set in appropriate places. The scenes and views produced by this architectural background were interesting and charming. The place at one time had been the domain of nobility and this was the setting for moonlight festivals. Greek plays were given here in which the guests represented mythological gods on Olympus. Standing there one could imagine the music made by Pan's pipes, lyres and cymbals coming over sweet-sented flowering shrubs, and the fountain from which the nymphs and dryads sprang out singing and dancing to be joined by groups of fauns and satyrs. It is a setting that stirs the imagination and makes one dream.

Another park is the unique Park Buttes-Chaumont, a most original and interesting park, and yet so little known. It is located on the northeast edge of the city, in the vicinity of La Villette, the stockyards. The grounds had formerly been a stone quarry. When the quarries were abandoned it became a city dump. Someone had a vision of all that good for nothing ground and eye-sore waste becoming a magnificent park for the enjoyment of the people of that locallity. It had been an unsightly hole in the ground with water at the bottom in which several lives had been lost, but when I approached this place I came upon a wide expanse of sloping green meadow. On it was an heroic bronze group representing a stone-age man carrying a helpless woman. A little farther there was another bronze group of a mother with a small child under one arm and the other hand helping an older child. A brook rippled down the sloping ground to its rocky bottom. Water plants and flowers grew all along the edge so you could follow its meandering course. Gradually the ground rose, and there behold, another heroic-size bronze group, a shepherd and his dog running down hill. More abruptly the ground rose to a knoll almost two hundred feet high with a growth of trees and shrubs upon it, and crowned with a beautiful vestal temple flanked by a few stately cypresses. There was another dramatic bronze group perched upon a projecting ledge, of a man battling an eagle. Gradually the scene changed as one descends into a chasm below. At the bottom of this seemingly natural depression is a good-sized lake. Around the shore is a panorama of changing scenes, of caves and grottos and waterfalls. A truly remarkable and imaginative park created out of a city dump. In the winter time when the lake was frozen I often went skating there with the daughter of my friends, the Hirsches.

Then of course, there is the Bois de Boulonge with its extensive forest beauty, and the Park Montsouris, noted for its great display of flowers and statuary. Statuary in parks, other than the display of art, adds so much to the enjoyment of nature.

So much beauty and so much to see in Paris: the glory of the Cathedral of Notre Dame, dating from the 13th Century; the Eiffel Tower, a wonder of colossal grace, built for the 1889 Exposition. Another masterpiece of purest Gothic architecture is the Tour St. Jacques, standing alone at the Place St. Jacques, surrounded by beautiful trees and flowers. Everywhere is statuary in perfectly designed settings.

The art-filled Pere-Lachaise Cemetary is another experience. Here the art touches the heart. P.A. Bartolome depicated this with great force in his original group of many figures carved out of one solid piece of colithic lime stone. It stands inside the entrance to the cemetary and is dedicated to the dead. The cemetary is a veritable outdoor museum of sculpture commemorating some of the great and illustrious citizens of France.

France has passed through many severe trials in her effort to better the environment for her citizens, and the principal method most fully utilized has been by means of things which can be seen, and that means art of all kinds.

At the great annual art exhibition, the first choice is purchased and placed in the Luxenbourg Museum where it remains for a period of ten or more years on trial. After that it may pass into the Louvre for perpetuity. If not destined for such an exalted place for permanent display, a place is found for it in some other museum. The subsidy to the artist is very generous.

Things went on as usual at the Beaux Arts. Nothing unusual transpired, just the usual routine, every two weeks a new male or female model posed. We built up our clay models, modeled, finished, tore down to start another. But we were taking stock of ourselves, working hard, always competing with each other. We were also making plans for the future.

The Chicago Columbian Exposition was then in the planning stage, and my friend Karl Bitter was superintendent of sculpture. We had become friends in Berlin. I was instrumental in getting him to America and was hopeful of getting work on the Exposition. My plans were made, but first I wanted to tour Italy, so I prepared to leave at the end of the semester when the weather was most favorable for travel.

There was one more place I wanted to visit before leaving Paris. My friend Sigwardt said I must see the Olympus, a restaurant where our gods, the great masters of art met for relaxation. It was a very humble little place, serving meals and wine. It had a front and a rear room a few steps below but not divided by a wall. The rear room was the larger, and was the rendezvous of our demigods. The Place was devoid of any display of art, perhaps in deference to their noted patrons. After basking in the sanctified atmosphere of the place and lingering over a glass of good French wine, we departed with a firm resolve to become great artists.

During my many visits with the Hirsches, I had failed to notice a growing attachment on the part of their daughter. When I came to say good-bye, to my great surprise she broke into such a flood of tears that it was necessary to explain the cause. It seems she had developed a romantic affection for me that I did not suspect. I was very touched and sorry, but I was innocent, and so I said farewell to my dear friends.

Chapter VI
Summer of 1891

Completing my studies in Paris, I started on the trip I had planned which would permit me to see and enjoy the magnificant works of the master artists of Italy.

I had purchased a three month Cook's Tours ticket, which would take me from Paris to Germany and on to Italy where I would visit all of the principal cities as far south as Naples, and return to Germany where I would sail from Hamburg to New York.

My first stop in Germany was at Wurzburg where Martin Luther was in hiding at the time he translated the Bible. I saw the famous spot where he had thrown his inkwell, supposedly at the Devil. The same day I was on my way to Nurnberg.

Nurnberg is an old city noted for its Medieval architecture, and the locale for Richard Wagner's "Die Meistersinger." It has a magnificant art museum filled with rare treasures; and anyone interested in knowing what civilization had to overcome, must visit the Seven Cornered Tower and see the exhibit of instruments of torture, the most ingenious and terrifying devices imaginable. Hell could have nothing so evil in design. There is one known as "The Iron Maiden." It is an over-sized, bulky-looking representation of a female figure made of sheet iron with an inner and an outer shell. It is divided in two parts, front and rear, with hinges on one side. It could be closed like a book and it had an arrangement by which the contraption could be slowly and securely closed. This "Maiden" was designed to receive a human being. The inside of the front section was studded with a number of sharp spikes, six inches or more long, corresponding in position to the vital organs, including eyes and mouth and lower parts of the body. There was, beneath this diabolical instrument of torture, a shaft or shute connected to it, and also studded with sharp projecting knives. The chute led to the river below. The floor upon which the victim stood was a trap door. After a lingering and horrible torture the victim's body was released through the chute where it was further mutilulated as it fell into the river to be carried away.

After coming from that chamber of horrors I felt a need for a stimulant, and soon found a tavern with a very interesting patio with heavy oak tables and chairs with backs carved with humorous figures. The pleasant environment and a stein of good cool beer with half of a large white radish, tasty rye bread with fresh butter, soon erased the effect of what I had seen. But man's inhumanity to man is something one never really forgets.

The next morning I left for Munich where I had a standing invitation from the mother of my friend Ludwig Voedermeier of Berlin student days. I was received graciously on my arrival and invited to be her guest while there. This made my week stay in Munich very delightful as she was a charming lady. I also enjoyed a performance of "Lohengrin" at the Royal Opera House. I took ample time to visit the great museum, the Schack Gallery, public buildings and fountains of which there were some of great artistic beauty.

Of no minor importance in Munich are its world famous breweries and the decorative Hoffbrau Houses and Rathskellers. The characters to be seen in them were most interesting. They are the "steadies" immune to intoxication. There seems to be no limit to the number of steins of beer they can consume, and wager to prove it.

From there my tour took me to Basel where I crossed the bridge to the Swiss side of the border and I visited a museum there. I then went to Lucerne, for I wanted to see the locality which Schiller made famous with his "William Tell." At Lucerne I saw the great double life-size statue of a lion created by Thorwaldsen, the Danish sculptor, which was in a remarkable setting between two buildings.

From there I went to Milan where the Milan cathedral, considered the seventh wonder of the world, is located. It is built of white marble, and the lavish amount of sculpture is staggering. Another sight I would not have missed under any circumstances was the Milan Cemetery with its extensive display of monuments and sculptures. It vies with that of Genoa for its collection. In Milan I also saw Leonardo da Vinci's al fresco painting of "The Last Supper" which sublimely lives up to its reputation of being one of the world's masterpieces. I stopped here overnight and called upon some people whose address had been given me by friends, so I had a pleasant evening.

My next stop was Turin where I saw a splendid plaza with Rococo statues. However, what impressed me most was the bizarre appearance of thousands of pigeons, dyed all colors of the rainbow. An additional proof, perhaps, of the Italian's love of color.

From here I went to Genoa with its historic background, where I recall the beautiful Campo Santo and a beautiful marble monument to Columbus.

These several stops had helped me get my bearings, and I realized I needed daylight to see all the things of interest, and the night to sleep, so I arranged to arrive in daylight, checked my luggage at the railroad station and looked for a hotel. Having found a hotel and a pleasant restaurant, I would spend the evening studying my Baedeker for the next day's adventure. This system worked out very satisfactorily on the entire trip. Travelling alone I had no interference with any plan I might wish and no other's desires or comfort had to be considered. I was so completely occupied I do not remember a moment of being lonely.

Seeing as much as possible was my purpose, as part of my art education, and yet I had to hurry with as little delay as possible for there was so much to see and I wanted to return home in time to work on the Chicago Columbian Exposition. I sometimes found it advantageous to leave the beaten path and lose myself on the outskirts of a town.

From Genoa I went to Pisa, for I wanted to see and go up in the famous Leaning Tower. Anyone who ascends the tower feels he is taking his life in his hands, and the sensation that climbing the steps creates is not unlike mal de mer. The tower is 179 feet high, and at that height was 13 feet out of plumb, and it is probably more now. Upon descending to solid ground it is with a feeling of thankfulness that one's life has been spared through some divine intercession.

The cathedral at Pisa was quite uninteresting, being commonplace and unfinished; a strange building in comparison with its famous camposanto.

An amusing incident occured here. As I went about the town I came upon a drinking fountain, and being tired and thirsty decided to have a drink. It was just a pump like those found on American farms. There was a group of urchins loitering about, and seeing a stranger decided they would collect tribute, so they barred my way to the fountain. Not caring to be held up by these boys, which is common in Italy, I pushed them aside and had my drink. The climax to this incident, however, came later that evening when I went into a restaurant. The food and drink was good and they had really good orchestral music. I sat at a long table and across from me was a family with several children including one of the boys at the fountain. Seeing me, and thinking to be smart, he told his father of the incident, and the father instead of thinking it funny became angry and reprimanded the boy who was chagrined. I understood little Italian, but I smiled across the table to assure them I was not angry, and so we enjoyed our meal.

The next morning found me on my way to Florence, which is a mecca for artists, and holds the thrill of thrills for every sculptor, for here the great master Michelangelo created most of his finest works.

First, I wanted to see the Logia Lanzi, an architectural gem with its important sculptures. Here is Benvenuto Cellini's bronze Mercury, Bernini's marble group The Rape of the Sabines, and another bronze statue by Donatello, of David with Goliath's head at his feet.

The Art Academy, which is about a block away, was the next place of interest, for here is Michelangelo's David as well as innumerable other important works.

I went next to Lorenzo di Medici's tomb, another of Michelangelo's masterpieces. There were many other places of interest including the galleries of Offizi, Accademio delle Belle Arti and the Bargello. These contain the works by Alesandro Rafaello, Andrea DelCarto, Botticelli, D. Ghirlandaio and Luca della Robbia among many others. The Bargello has a Sala di Donatello which is a museum of all his works including his St. George, St. Giovani and David. At the St. Giovani Baptistry the north and south gates are by Lorenzo Ghiberti.

The great wealth of art made my stay in Florence an extraordinary experience for there were so many masterpieces of sculpture. Dominating them all, throughout the city, was to be seen the results of Michelangelo's genius; and to enjoy and appreciate them to the fullest they must be seen in their natural setting.

I took a short side trip by cog-wheel railway to Fiesole, which had an interesting shrine and monastery, and a most magnificant view of the city. I could not spare more than a day on the art treasures of Florence, so the next day found me on my way to Rome.

I stayed in Rome for two weeks. I arrived in the evening and my first effort was to find an address a friend had given me as a possible place to stay. I found it was a boarding house which pleased me, but later considered it the one regretable experience of my entire trip.

Having found the place I knocked on the door and noticed it was only dimly lighted. After a time someone came to the door and opened it rather furtively. This person hesitated about letting me in, and with all the jabbering in Italian I finally understood the place had been closed by the sheriff. However, I insisted upon being permitted to stay the night for I had no desire to hunt another place at night. Finally I was permitted to enter and was given a room. These rooms were simply partitions which divided a large room, and the partitions did not rise to the ceiling. I became increasingly uneasy as I thought I had probably gotten into a den of thieves. I heard various voices all through the night from the other rooms, for I was unable to sleep, being awake killing bedbugs and fleas. The only illumination was a candle on a table. I left very early in the morning, feeling lucky to get out without being robbed.

I set out to find another address which had been given to me by Karl Weber, a fellow student in Berlin. I found that he was now living here with a German who had a gift shop and rented rooms. He was able to accommodate me, and I was given a clean and pleasant room.

I found the two weeks I had in Rome was very limited for there was so much to see. One of the most impressive places is the acres of marble sculpture in the Vatican Museum which beggers discription. I saw them all and was exhausted.

Naturally, I visited St. Peter's Cathedral, both inside and out. It is staggering in beauty and dimension. I recall the spacious plaza, and as I walked across it at noon the heat was overpowering. I could well understand why Italians, like natives of other warm climates take a noontime siesta.

On the monument to Pope Julius II is Michelangelo's impressive figure of Moses. I was anxious to see the Sistine Chapel, and I was enormously impressed by the supreme genius of Michelangelo. He was a man equally great in sculpture, painting and architecture. He designed St. Paul's magnificant dome. It is incomprehensible that one man was able to create and carry out a body of work of such magnitude.

The Sistine Chapel is awe-inspiring. The tremendous ceiling and wall-space covered literally with thousands of figures of incomparable workmanship and artistry. To make it even more awesome, we must remember that this work was done al fresco, that is directly on a fresh lime stucco which is prepared and applied daily on the area to be worked on that day, and the entire section must be completed that day as the pigments react with the lime and there can be no working over. It is a demonstration of great skill and of the tremendous love this genuis had for his art. It becomes even more impressive when we remember that in order to carry out this work of unerring workmanship, it was necessary for him to paint most of it while lying flat on his back on scaffolding high above the floor of the chapel. It was with real regret I had to leave this shrine, but there was so much for me to see during my brief stay.

My next point of interest was the Colosseum, that huge structure which has stood for over 2000 years. It had also been created by skilled artists and builders; considering the period when it was built it is even more impressive. We are reminded of the cataclysmic vicissitudes of history that this structure has withstood and we still marvel that so much of it still remains for us to admire. I felt it was a great privilege to walk over this ground and recall the historical scenes which were enacted here.

The remains of the ancient Roman civilization are so numerous in this beautiful city that it is impossible to mention all of the treasures which I enjoyed. The magnificant structure of the Pantheon seemed to be the most perfectly preserved. I remember especially Trajan's Column, the Arch of Titus and some impressive remains of the Diocletian public baths, and those of Caracalla whose interior is well preserved, with a gem of a marble statue of a kneeling boy without head or arms, which must have been done by one of the great ancient sculptors.

Yes, I was on the Appian Way, and saw the well-preserved stone road which the ancient Romans laid down, which give at least as good service as the modern roads, and off in the distance I saw the remains of the celebrated acqueduct.

Outside of Rome there are a number of scenic places from which I selected to spend a day, Fradcati and Tivoli the ancient city of the Tibur, which was noted for its ancient Roman villas and temple of Vestrus.

When I arrived at Tivoli I found I was on the edge of a deep gorge opposite the temples, so I started to walk down the steep side. At the bottom I heard a donkey braying and was soon approached by a man who had trained the donkey to warn him of the approach of a stranger. He wanted me to hire him to carry me up the other side, which I refused but later regretted, for when I reached the top I found my shoes needed new soles.

As I had already spent a week of intense sight-seeing in Rome I decided a change of scene would be beneficial. As Naples, Pompeii and Paestum were on my itinerary, I decided to take four or five days to see them.

I kept my room and arranged to have some much-needed laundry done during my absence, and taking a small bag which would take care of my needs for the few days, I took the train for Naples.

In European trains the cars have a long corridor running down one side of the car with compartments opening off this passage in which the passengers ride. The compartments are fitted with two seats which face each other and accommodate four to six persons on each side. This arrangement is conducive to conversations among the occupants, and I was soon talking to a gentleman who seemed anxious to talk. He was visably agitated, very worried about his safety, having heard much about the violence and banditry of the Italians, and their use of the stiletto. He expected to meet a bandit at any minute. He was Finnish, and part of his concern was because he was travelling with a very elderly uncle and aunt and he feared for their lives.

After a time he inquired about my plans and then inquired if I had engaged a hotel in Naples. When I told him I had not but would have no difficulty finding a place after I arrived, he was amazed. He told me he had engaged rooms at the Hotel Hassler, which claimed to be the finest hotel in the city. I told him frankly that such a place was beyond my travel budget. He became very apologetic and insisted "I am asking you to be my guest, and it will cost you nothing." "Such generosity," I told him, "no artist could refuse, and, being an artist, I will accept." He was delighted and we shook hands to seal the offer. He acted as though a great weight had been lifted from his shoulders for I think he saw me as a bodyguard.

Our acquaintance grew very pleasantly until we reached Naples. At the station we were bombarded by young girls selling flowers, and my friend purchased some and then we took a carriage to the hotel. Our way took us on a drive along the seashore which reminded me of the Lake Shore drive in Chicago. Arriving at the hotel we were given very pleasant rooms with a view of the park and sea. Below in the plaza a string trio consisting of a harp, mandolin and violin were playing. I remember Santa Lucia sounded especially appropriate. The musicians were well rewarded with a shower of coins from my friend, for which they favored us with an encore. After this interlude we enjoyed a delicious dinner with several excellent wines, in a private dining room. After dinner we escorted the old couple to their room and we went out to see the city and some of its night life.

We took a cab to one of the better music halls where we saw some excellent performers and had a few more drinks. It struck me that the entertainment was much the same and comparable to that which we had at home. After a little more walking around we returned to the hotel and to sleep after an interesting day.

The next day was devoted to a trip to the Isle of Capri with tremendous cliffs which rise directly from the sea to a height of 900 feet. This famous jewel off the coast of Naples, was reached after a steamer trip of about two hours. Then small boats take the passengers to the famous Blue Grotto and to see the remains of the ancient Roman baths which can be seen beneath the surface of the clear water.

The entrance to the Grotto is through a small passage which is so low one must almost lie in the bottom of the boat to pass under the overhanging rocks. Once inside, the space is huge and everything is colored an indescribable blue from the reflected light from the water which is wonderfully clear in spite of the coloration. Small boys dove into the water to retrive coins tossed for them, and you could see them all the way to the bottom, a depth of about 50 feet.

When we returned to the town we left the old couple and went out to see the other sights, one of which was the ancient Villa di Tiberio, a rather extensive Roman ruin which at this time was being used as a cow shed. We picked up his aunt and uncle and went to a most picturesque little ivy-covered cottage restaurant with a beautiful view, where we enjoyed another fine dinner. We took the return vessel to Naples and back to the hotel with plans for a trip to Pompeii scheduled for the next day.

In the morning a carriage was hired for the fifteen mile ride through many interesting little villages including Terro del Greko and Ressina which is built at the top of Herculaneum. We also saw macaroni being made and drying in the sun on long racks along the roadside. Shirtless men were moving along them turning and changing the racks.

Our trip had the added interest of coinciding with a local religious festival, and every village we passed had erected an alter made of colored paper, flowers, tinsel and candles. The celebration was to start at sundown.

When we arrived in Pompeii we rested a short time at the hotel then went about inspecting the ruins, which was a great experience, especially to anyone who had read Bulwer-Lytton's "Last Days of Pompeii" which gave life to the scene, remembering the hero Glaucus, whose house was pointed out by the guide; and the heroine, the blind flower girl, Nydia. However, my friends did not show more than a perfunctory interest in the ruins, being more tiring to them than entertaining.

After eating and drinking once again, we returned to Naples which took us through the villages where the religious festival was in progress, consisting of a procession of priests blessing the parishioners and village, to the accompaniment of singing, dancing and fireworks.

In one of the villages we found ourselves surrounded by the surging mass of celebrants, all of them in festive mood. We were rather bewildered as we did not know what it was about, and as the crowds gathered around we began to feel that we were the cause of the celebration. It was an enjoyable entertainment we had not anticipated. Fortune being on my side, as guardian of these kind people from Finland, we arrived back at the hotel in Naples about midnight, safe and sound and not one stilleto had been seen.

I had enjoyed my experience with these new and generous friends, but the interlude did not belong on my schedule, and I had done no browsing in art. So when I went to the railway station with them the next morning I thanked them and wished them a safe journey home. The young man was a professor of languages, and that is all I know about him. I am sorry to say, that at this distance in time, I do not even remember his name.

Henceforth I was on my own, and once again with my trusty Baedeker in my pocket, I set out to resume my tour of the wonders of the world of art.

I remembered having passed an aquarium in the seaside park, so I stopped there and for the first time saw a real live octopus and the cunning little sea horses. After this enjoyable respite I located the Naples Museum which contains most of the treasures of Herculaneum and Pompeii. Herculaneum yielded treasures, the equal of any in the world. Copies of these rare bronzes and marbles were reproduced and now grace most of the museums of the world. The original of the Laocoon group is here. The museum also contains a library of 3000 rolls of papyrus which were found there. After seeing these treasures I decided to return to Pompeii. This time I would be alone and could take time to savor this historic place.

Going there this time by train, I arrived in late afternoon and obtained a room in a very nice hotel across the road from the ruins of ancient Pompeii. The gates to the enclosure were locked so I spent the evening at the hotel. A group of about a dozen German tourists entered, and it was a pleasure to feel their enthusiasm for the romance of Pompeii after the indifference of my Finnish friends, and to be able to understand what they were saying, for my Italian was still very limited.

The next morning I was on my way to Paestum by train. The only thing of interest along the way were the many water buffalo standing in water to keep off the insect pests. That reminded me we had been warned of the prevalence of malaria in this country which accounted for the abandonment of this ancient civilization dating as far back as the 6th Century, B.C. or even earlier.

The train arrived at Paestum about noon, and I was the only passenger to get off. The station master, a small fellow, received me joyously, all but embracing me. His pleasure seemed to be related to food, for he had a few words of English, and he kept repeating "Beefsteak." I was at a loss to comprehend where such fare could come from for I saw no evidence of anything to eat. All I saw was a very small shack which served as the station, and there was no restaurant in sight. With my meagre Italian I gave him to understand a couple of sandwiches with a little wine would do nicely. I left the procurement of these items to his own device, for I had already noticed that the temples were about a block away. I assertained when the next train would arrive to take me back to Pompeii and set out to be inspired by one of the world's greatest architectural masterpieces, the Temple of Neptune.

It is generally conceded that outside of Athens, the Temple of Neptune is the finest example of Greek architecture. It is in the Doric style, and had not been mutilated in any way. However, numerous sculptural pieces had been carried away from this lonely place. This area had been a Greek colony, and during the early centuries had changed many times, finally coming under the rule of the Romans who held it until the fall of the Roman Empire.

It was very hot the day I visited Paestum, and I sought the shelter of one of the huge columns of the temple. Meanwhile, my station master arrived with the welcome repast of sandwiches and a bottle of wine, which I shared with him.

A second temple, that of Ceres, which I saw at some distance was of a later period and of inferior quality to that of Neptune, and I did not visit it.

The heat was intense, and the only shade was the temple which was filled with insects, probably carrying the Maleria germ, but I never gave it a thought as I was lost in reverie in this beautiful place. My reverie was interrupted by two urchins who wanted to sell me some pieces of pottery shards as antiques, whose authenticity was very dubious. I had the pleasure of meeting two artists, also from the United States, who were here for the same reason as I. They were seeing the country on foot which is really the only way to see everything.

At about three o'clock in the afternoon the train arrived which would take me back to Pompeii. It was made up of fourth class cars only, simple freight cars with a bench all around the inside, and it was loaded to capacity with standing room only. I was fortunate, however, in finding a seat, fortunately alongside an open window for the heat and body odor was overpowering as the other passengers were apparently farm laborers. The journey took three hours which seemed like an eternity, but we finally arrived at my beloved Pompeii.

The next day I was to ascend Vesuvius. I never considered that there might be any danger or difficulty. Of course, I realized I would need a guide, as a matter of fact, I was obliged to hire two.

We went by horseback as far as the horses could travel, and then we went by foot, with the guides helping me over the large boulders and steep ground. The higher we climbed the colder and windier it became. The cracks in the lava were emitting smoke and sulphur fumes. About half way we came upon a grotto, occupied by one of the guide's associates who had wine to sell, and I was pursuaded to understand that my very existence depended upon my drinking wine. So I arbitrated the argument and bought a bottle of La Creme Cristi, one of the most celebrated Italian wines, and which I will admit was excellent. I had little resistance to wine, and so I let my guides drink most of it for the little I drank at that altitude, was more than was good for me. We were then about 4000 feet altitude with a strong wind blowing, sulphur fumes rising and a very hot sun beating down on us, as well as the heat from the volcano, so I needed all my fortitude.

After this interlude we started out again with the guides pushing and pulling me over the rough places. With extreme exertion we finally arrived at the crater's rim which had ample space on it to walk around the crater which was about 100 feet in diameter. The interior was bowl-shaped and not too deep, with several fumeroles at the bottom.

My guides now suggestd another gentle hold-up, asking for a few centimes which they would embed in molten lava. I considered this favorably as a souvenir, and gave them a couple of lira for their trouble.

After seeing the mighty Vesuvius and enjoying the spectacular view, came the final test, to negotiate the Devil's Slide. At a short distance from the top there is a very steep decline of about 1000 feet, composed of volcanic ash, soft and clear. The guide said I should sit on this ash, he doing the same at my side. We leaned back, wiggled a bit to get started, and then down we went, going like the wind. You can control yourself a little by digging your hands and feet into the ash. We made the descent without mishap, but today I tremble at the very thought of it.

We soon met our mounts and so back to the hotel without further incident, for a much needed bath and change of clothes. As the horseback ride had been the first in my life it was lucky the horse needed no guiding on my part, and I used all my effort just to hold on as he travelled at a rapid pace. That night I was so stiff and sore that I ate my dinner in the proverbial manner of "standing at the mantle."

The next day I went to worship at the shrine of antiquity. I spent the entire day among the ruins of this dead city with a guide so I would be sure not to miss anything. One cannot escape the impression that Pompeii was a city of advanced culture and riches. It was a port city with a population of more than 30,000 that had an amphitheater seating 20,000 people, another theater of 5,000 seats, and yet another seating 1,500. There was a temple to Fortuna, another to Isis, and one to Apollo. There were also two Thermes (baths): Stabina and Nigidea Vaccula, which were beautiful creations.

In all physicial respects we had far to go to improve upon what they had so many centuries before us. They used lead pipes for plumbing, heating was accomplished by conducting it through hollow tiles in the floors and walls, as well as the use of braziers in which charcoal burned.

Everything in this city was preserved by the fine ash from the eruption of Vesuvius in 79 A.D. We came upon a bakery where we saw the mill and ovens, even some of the loaves of bread. At the entrance of this shop there were two pedestals upon which marble statues had stood, and are now in the Naples Museum for safe keeping, as are many other treasures from Pompeii. There were olive oil and wine presses, and a donkey still harnessed to his cart. There was also a market for garden and farm produce. One of the streets of the city has been named the "Street of Tombs" because of the number of marble memorials lining it. Buildings were identified by symbolic paintings on the walls, or by mosaics. The streets in general, were named after mythological characters and the same applied to the wall paintings. There was hardly a house that was not decorated with wall paintings or mosaics, and at the thresholds or front doors were often to be found beautiful mosaics with various motifs ranging from a sleeping dog to the single word "Peace" as welcome, surrounded by a decorative design. There were many large villas with patios, peristyles and fountains.

My guide led me to a house with a tragic story. Here in a large vaulted basement had been found the skeletons of nineteen women and children, their heads wrapped in cloths which had failed to save them from being suffocated by the penetrating fine volcanic ash which had buried the city. At the top of the stairs the remains of a bearded man had been found, still holding a key in his hand.

The ash deposit, saturated with rain water through the nineteen centuries before the city was uncovered, had been coverted into a form of cement which made a mold of the objects it enveloped. From these molds very good facsimilies were made in plaster of the entrapped citizens, so an exact reproduction of the city on the day of the disaster was possible.

The guide pointed out to me a plot of ground where the remains of a gladiator's barracks had been found with the paraphernalia which was part of their calling. Also, a skeleton in stocks had been found, with a chain still holding it.

This so-called "dead city" stimulates the imagination. For the most part, the remains of antiquity baffle our ability to understand the men who created them, but here we have the remains not only of the objects, but also those who fashioned them, all in their original place. Here we have a city of people, frozen into immobility in the midst of their normal occupations and activities. Thus, we are able to understand them much better than we have been able to perceive other ancient civilizations.

The toll of dead discovered in the excavations numbered over two thousand persons. There had been an earthquake in 63 A.D. which did much damage, but it has been said that the eruption of Vesuvius on August 24, 79 A.D. was a catastrophe so overwhelming that although some survivors returned to attempt to dig the ash away from their property, and to find missing family and friends, the task was too much, and they had to give up their efforts.

So Pompeii, deserted, retained its secrets until excavations were begun in 1748. It was with a heavy heart and deep sympathy that I said farewell to Pompeii and returned to Naples where I received some much needed attention from a barber. The barbers had a side vocation. When not attending patrons they were busy fashioning mosaic jewelry. I purchased several sets of cuff links from them. I was told the delicate work seriously affected their eyesight, and I wondered what risk their customers were taking in being shaved with their long straight-edge razors.

Being much refreshed after my shave and a luncheon of the usual macaroni, I returned once more, for a last look at the Naples Museum which lists over 200,000 items and spent the rest of the day enjoying the wonders it contains.

Again I was on a train, on my way back to Rome, and although I still had numerous places to go and things I wanted to see, my trip home had started.

Arriving in Rome I returned to my old headquarters which I had retained. The people had started to worry for I had overstayed my trip to Pompeii. They spoke only French, and were interested and amazed at the number of places I had been and the things I had seen. I was happy to be able to carry on a conversation with people who understood me and I could understand, for I never did master the Italian language.

I spent two or three days in Rome, and once again saw Trajan's Column, that beautiful shaft of marble which rises almost 150 feet. I was again impressed by the genius of the ancient Romans, for this column is constructed of eighteen huge drums of marble, each about five feet high, with diameter of ten or eleven feet. The column stands upon a pedestal and surmounting it is a statue, originally of Trajan who was buried beneath it, but later replaced by a statue of Saint Peter. Around the column is a spiral band about three feet wide, carved in relief with thousands of human figures depicting Trajan's war with the Dacians. Up through the interior of the column there rises a spiral staircase, carved out of the solid marble, I wondered how they were able to carve these stairs, and the method they used; a very impressive and remarkable achievement.

The ancient Roman forum was another construction which impressed me very much, but there have been so many new excavations since I was there with consequent magnificent discoveries, that I feel descriptions of what I saw might proved inadequate or even misleading, for some of the places I saw have even been renamed. I did not go to see the catacombs as I had planned, as they were not important in my schedule. I did, however, go down into St. Peter's dungeon where he converted and baptised his guard. A small chapel protects this ancient shrine.

I invited my artist colleague, Karl Weber, to join me for my last dinner in Rome. We went to the celebrated restaurant where good orchestral music and opera enhanced the enjoyment of the food. It was frequented by numerous cardinals from the Vatican who enjoyed the good food and operetic music.

When I returned to my rooms I completed preparations for my departure, and settled my bills. The next day I took my Cooks Tours ticket to the railway station for the necessary validation and was soon on my way to Bologna. I had no intention of stopping here overnight as it would take only a few hours to see what was of interest to me. This was the magnificent fountain of Neptune in marble and bronze. A fine work of art, well worth seeing. Another sight I wanted to see was a freak of three leaning towers with no artistic merit, and barring the vista as they protrude into almost every view. I was soon on my way again, with my next stop Verona.

The scenery along the way was of argicultural country, similar to that along almost any railway line, with occasionally a vista which reminded one of the history of this country which was frequently ravaged by war, completely destroying city after city down through the centuries, such as Aquila, Altinum, Concorbine, Padua and even Verona.

My main purpose in visiting Verona was to see the city made famous by the world's greatest love story, "Romeo and Juliet," immortalized by Shakespeare, and to see Juliet's house which still stands. Entrance to the house is made through a large gate which is identified by an escutcheon of Capulet. The house stands in a large courtyard which, when I was there, was filled with donkeys, horses and drays indicating the place might be a rooming-house. Around the entire second story of the house is the balcony upon which the romantic balcony scene took place. Not far, across the street, I found the marble trough, a watering place for horses, which was once supposed to have held the remains of poor Juliet.

I took a short walk before dinner and found a small fenced-in aquare with a group of beautiful medieval monuments. I returned to Juliet's house to have something to eat and to stay overnight and dream of Juliet. The next morning I was on my way to the fairy city of Venice, built all of marble.

My first concern on arriving in Venice was to find lodging for three or four days. I checked my bags at the station and sallied forth to put to the test that one can go anywhere in Venice without using the waterways. By the time I found a satisfactory lodging and a good place to eat it was getting dusk. Soon the city of marble and marvels would be bathed in a golden sunset so I retrieved my luggage and took a gondola to my hotel. I had my dinner at once for I did not want to be out after dark where all of the streets are water, and the lighting very feeble. I had no occasion to partake of the night life of Venice, not knowing anyone in the city. As I needed daylight for my excursions I took as much rest as I could after dark and rose early in the morning.

The first day was a full one for I had decided to see the Lido and the American Monastery. The weather was beautiful and so far I was in luck, for I had not had a drop of rain on my entire journey.

The Lido is an island bathing resort, a strip of dunes a half mile wide by seven miles long, and is one of the islands that act as a breakwater between Venice and the Adriatic Sea. It boasted one horsecar to carry passengers to the various sandy beaches.

The Monastery, to which one donates a lire in order to enter, was on another island which is reached by a small steamer. It is a very fertile and beautiful spot and the Brothers spend most of their time tending to their truck-gardens and vineyards. The head of the monastery was a tall and handsome man with jet black hair and dark eyes. He was very vocal, and an excellent linguist who spoke several languages including English, German and French. The day had passed very pleasantly and I felt refreshed. The return trip afforded a magnificant view of the Piazza de San Marco where we debarked.

One cannot escape the attraction and fascination of the Piazza San

Marco. I find it difficult to describe it adequately, and as it has been done so much better than anything I could say, by such writers as Lord Byron, John Ruskin, Elizateth Barrett Browning among others I shall not attempt to do so; but here is a brief quotation from Howell's "Venetian Life."

"The place of St. Mark is the heart of Venice, and from this beats new life in every direction through the intricate system of streets and canals, that bring it back again to the same center. . . Of all the open space in the city, that before the Church of St. Mark alone bears the name Piazza, and the rest are called merely campi or fields. But if the company of the noblest architecture can give honor, the Piazza of St. Marco merits its distinction, not in Venice only, but in the whole world. . . . "The church which the mighty bell tower and the lofty height of the palace lines make to look low, is in no way humbled by the contrast but is like a queen enthroned amid upright reverence."

One truly stands in awe in this place, not only for its beauty but for its history.

I adhered to my usual practice, and saw Venice on foot, using gondolas only when it was absolutely necessary. As usual, walking affords glimpses of things not otherwise seen. As I was admiring the statue of Bartolomeo Colleoni, the most famous equestrain monument in the world, my attention was drawn to a small church in back of the monument where a door was opening. At the same time three gondolas silently approached and stopped at the church. One had a catafalque, and was splendidly equipped; the front bore a golden lion holding a shield upon which was another winged lion, the symbol of St. Mark. All three gondolas had canopies of crimson plush with the side draperies drawn back and held by golden ropes. The gondoliers were dressed in Renaissance period costumes. A small procession emerged from the open church door. There were four pages dressed in the fashion of the Renaissance carrying a coffin, followed by several priests in their robes which were agitated by a slight breeze. Following them were four or five mourners. The coffin was placed on the catafalque and the priests and mourners took their places in the other gondolas, and silently as they arrived they departed. My eyes followed them until they disappeared in the mist in the direction of the Campo Santo, like a scene from an ancient drama, leaving me wondering if I had dreamed what I had just seen.

Then my attention went back to the Bartolomeo Colleoni monument. He is seated upright in a richly ornamented saddle, turning slightly and looking over his left shoulder. This work was started by the sculptor Andrea del Verrocchio, but upon his sudden death it was completed by Alessandro Leopardi.

Of the various bridges over the canals, all of which are more or less similar, there are two of particular interest: the Realto and the Bridge of Sighs. The Realto is a large bridge, unique among bridges for it is not only a covered bridge which spans a waterway, it is also a building which contains many shops and vendor's stalls. It is a lively mart where the Venetians shop and use as a meeting place, and where artists find many of their models. The Bridge of Sighs serves a far different purpose. It spans a narrow canal between the Doge's Palace and the Piombi Dungeons. It is said that whoever passed over this bridge had taken his last walk, and thus with a sigh, had given up his last hope of freedom.

During his thirty-five years of incarceration in these dungeons Casanova, the famous prisoner, wrote of his thoughts and experiences; and Lord Byron spent twenty-four hours in one of them in order to express his feelings in his impressive poem.

The Council of Ten, who sat in the Doge's Palace, was infamous for the unjust decisions it handed down, and yet they must be credited with a share of the beauty they helped create, although much of it was paid for in grief and blood.

While most churches have famous masterpieces, the church of Santa Maria della Salute probably has more masterpieces than any other. The Academia comes next, and the Muses Statuario has some fine sculpture. The artists whose work is represented in these three buildings are known throughout the world. including Tintoretto, who painted the Marriage of Cana, a picture that is twenty-five feet wide and fifteen feet high, Paolo Veronese, Tiepolo, Titian, Palla Vashio, Bonifacio I, II and III, and Bellini. These men all had patrons who kept them busy during their entire lifetime, leaving an unmatched legacy.

The Campanille is a masterpiece by Sansovino. This tower was started in the 8th Century and completed in the 15th. It boasted the celebrated bronze doors by Ghiberti. I was fortunate to see it, for it collapsed on July 14, 1902. The tower was rebuilt upon a firmer foundation and the bells and other objects which were destroyed were replaced.

I went back to the Piazza for one last time. I had already visited the interior of the Doge's Palace, and since I had been greatly impressed by St. Mark's Church, I went back to see the entrance with its brilliantly colored gold and glass mosaic background. Even at the time of this writing I am still impressed by the memory of its never fading beauty.

On the left side of the Piazza there is a long collonade in connection with a building containing a solid line of shops and a first class restaurant which includes tables set out of doors so you can enjoy a meal or a drink and watch the passing crowd and the pigeons. The shops were interesting. In one of them you could watch men blowing glass to make ornaments while you waited, a favorite attraction for tourists. There were, also, antique, mosaic and art stores where you could purchase genuine antique paintings as well as modern works. There was a book store with thousands of rare volumes and manuscripts with an aura of the important part they played in history. These shops offered a veritable heaven for collectors in which to browse.

This day was June 4, my father's birthday. After lunching at the outdoor cafe I hailed a gondola to return to my hotel and took my last view of this magic city, as I planned to leave the next day.

Once again I was on a train, regretfully bidding farewell to this land of culture, art and sunshine. Travelling north to Austria, we went through a mountain pass alternating darkness and light as we passed through at least a dozen long tunnels. This alternating of tunnels and open spaces continued for hours, until at last we reached Innsbruck.

I checked my luggage at the station and set out to see the town at my leisure. The cathedral is the only structure of any importance, and it is noted for several magnificent sculptural pieces. One was a white marble tomb, an elaborate sarcophagus with a carved marble figure lying on top. This was executed by an Irish sculptor named Collins. There were eight bas-relief panels on its sides which were done in a very realistic style including fine perspective. They represented historic events of Austrian royalty. I have never seen finer work. There were also, two bronze statues in the church which are unsurpassed in design and workmanship. One was an over life-sized figure of William the Conqueror, clothed in the most magnificent armor, which was covered with finely modeled figures, some of which were only two inches in size. The other was not unlike that of Michelangelo, short and stocky. He was covered from his neck to his feet in a leather apron. It was an interesting concept.

Innsbruck is situated at the base of a gigantic slab of rock at least 500 feet high, of a very dark color, which serves as an impressive backdrop for the city. There was no more of interest for me to see here and I was soon on my way to Berlin.

Arriving in Berlin, I was met by my very good friend Ludwig Vordermeier, to whom I had telegraphed the time of my arrival, and with whom I planned to stay for a few days.

We had much to say to each other about our experiences and, after depositing my luggage at his lodging, we decided to celebrate my homecoming as it were, at our favorite restaurant. It is strange how even a slight interval of time makes such a great difference in the viewpoint of people. We almost seemed like strangers, as if we had to renew our friendship. Our interests in life had undergone changes and our past student interests could not be regained in the face of our new experiences and concentration on the future, so we only had pleasant memories to recall.

I was anxious to move on to the new field of activity for which I had prepared myself. Ludwig's future was assured as he attached himself more firmly to his uncle Mathias, the finest marble sculptor in Berlin. In the meantime we had a very pleasant dinner, and we became sentimental in the course of our philosophising, pondering the uncertainties of life and the future.

It was vacation time for the students, but Ludwig managed to contact some of the fellows I had known, so on the day of my departure I had quite a group to see me off. Ludwig, always having a bit of deviltry in mind, had fashioned a wreath of straw with which to crown me for my accomplishment in art. While this jollification was going on a man stopped by as we hailed each other. He was an Englishman I had met on the train to Switzerland from Italy. He was returning to England, and I to the United States. The train was almost ready to start as I said a last sentimental farewell to my friends and to my happy student days.

Hamburg was the last train stop, and here I took the ship for home after three years of rewarding study and travel in Europe. The ocean voyage was uneventful and I stayed mostly by myself, contemplating my experiences and looking forward in hope and expectation to my future life.

Richard W. Bock — 1895-99

Chapter VII
1891-1893

It was late summer of 1891. I was twenty-six years of age, back in New York, prepared and eager to prove myself.

Returning to Chicago, I saw my family, and catching up on over three years away, I wasted no time in making contacts for work. I found that all of the contracts for sculpture on the World's Columbian Exposition had been assigned. There were, however some separate areas. The Phillipson Company was contracted to do the Mining and Metalurgy Building and the Electricity Building for the Fair. S.S. Beman was the architect who was designing both of these buildings and I contacted him, with the result I did the sculpture for both buildings.

The Electricity Building had a large pediment, and the Mining and Metalurgy Building huge spandrels and several figures. I received a medal as one of the designers of the Fair, and I was told afterward that the sculptor St. Gaudens, considered my work as among the best of the Fair.

One day, while at work, a sculptor, a Frenchman by the name of Wagner, showed me a circular for a competition for a bronze group atop the Library building in Indianapolis, Indiana. Asking if I knew about it he said he would not compete and I might keep the information. Reading it I found there was a joker as there often is in competitions when the awards committee has already made up its mind but legally has to hold an open competition. In this case, three sculptors had been invited to submit entries and had each been paid three hundred dollars for their

Mining Building, World's Columbian Exposition

44

Mining Building model with R.W. Bock

time and effort: Lorado Taft, Johannes Gellert and George Brewster. Anyone else was welcome to participate. There was only one week left to complete the whole task and deliver it. I hesitated, but my friendly French colleague was so convinced of my ability he was sure I couldn't lose. After careful consideration I decided to enter, and to my happy surprise my model was accepted over the invited sculptors.

My first studio was located in the Chicago loop on Wabash Avenue near Van Buren. This was one of the early Chicago buildings and was occupied by a number of artists. One of them, Arthur Feudel, told me confidentially, that he had been given a contract for a large mural painting for the Schiller Theater Building then under construction. He had seen the blue prints and they showed a considerable amount of sculpture about the stage. He recommended me for the work to the president of the Schiller Theater Building, Anton C. Hessing. He said I was to call Mr. Hessing as he said he would like to meet me. I should mention that Anton C. Hessing was a very influential person among the large German speaking population in Chicago, and was a formidable political power in the city. He was the editor of the Illinois Staats-Zeitung newspaper, and his son was a postmaster.

Mr. Hessing was pleased with my presentation and asked me to go to see Mr. Louis H. Sullivan, the eminent architect of the Schiller Building. I was to tell Mr. Sullivan that Mr. Hessing had sent me. This I did immediately, showing him my portfolio and references. Sullivan was very brusque. He refused to look at my pictures, brushing it all aside as of no consequence. I closed my portfolio and left, surprised by his lack of tact.

I speeded back to Mr. Hessing to recount to him my experience with

Indianapolis Library Group in situ

45

Mr. Sullivan. He looked at me, bit his lip, took his hat and said "Let us go over and see Mr. Sullivan." We were soon back in Mr. Sullivan's office. Hessing asked me to hand my photos to Mr. Sullivan. Mr. Hessing then asked Mr. Sullivan if he had seen my portfolio, and Mr. Sullivan replied "No, they are of no importance." "Well, I'll read the clippings to you then," said Mr. Hessing as he put the photographs on the desk. When Mr. Sullivan finally had an opportunity to speak, he asked Mr. Hessing "Do you want Mr. Bock to do this work?" Mr. Hessing answered without hesitation "Yes, I do." With that Mr. Sullivan directed me to go to the drafting-room and see Mr. Wright who would furnish me with blue prints and explain them to me. Contracts and specifications would be mailed. Going into the drafting-room I had my first meeting with Frank Lloyd Wright.

With my instructions, I returned to my studio to study the requirements and make sketches and models which took a number of days. Then I again returned to Mr. Sullivan's office to show him my prepared studies. He was very pleased and satisfied with them and made no criticism. To show that he wanted to be friendly he took out his own portfolio and showed me some of his precious designs, which were creative gems.

I could now go ahead with the execution of the works I had modeled, which consisted of two large tympanum at each side of the stage, flanked on either end with spandrels which were in low relief. These panels were filled with bold relief, one representing Homer reading his immortal verses; the other representing Schiller astride Pegasus, which is being led by Genius holding aloft a torch and guiding the way. The spandrels representing Strength and Beauty are on one side, those on the other represented Art and Music.

These elements on each side of the proscenium were supported by caryatid lions, while in the boxes were life-sized statues of children representing Morning, Noon, Evening and Night, each standing on a pedestal.

The size of the tympanum from side to side between the two caryatid lions was approximately eighteen feet. The headroom from the floor was seven feet. The tympanum contained six figures each. It was my desire to make the effort a worthy one, and I had models pose for all of the figures.

In the panel of Homer there was a group of two figures, male and female. The female leaning against the male figure, resting her folded hands in his lap as she listens enraptured to his verses. It was a difficult pose and was accomplished with some exertion by the model.

The work was well enough along to call for an inspection by the architect. Mr. Sullivan sent Frank Wright to shoulder the responsibility. He was a breezy young man, well groomed, with a definite self-assurance that was no doubt indicative of his destiny. He admired my work and his inspection was very satisfactory. He lingered, and I wondered if that was due to my accomplishments or to the posing model. I believe he came once more, and then we did not meet again for some time.

There was a frantic effort to complete the Schiller Theater Building in time for the scheduled opening of the theater. My panels were in place and the painters had completed their work of giving them an ivory finish, and the scaffolding was down. For me this was a private unveiling of my artistic effort, and I had many compliments for the work. The murals were in place, the seats installed, and there was the customary hustle and bustle of last minute activity.

While absorbed in viewing my work I was brought out of my reverie by an argument on the stage between Mr. Hessing, Mr. Sullivan and Mr. Temple, the lessee of the theater who was objecting about the boxes being cluttered up with statuary. For him, the chair space was of intrinsic value and much more important than the aesthetics of art.

Mr. Hessing asked me if I could design something as a supporting medium in place of the lions, and I answered off-hand that it could be done if it would satisfy all concerned. Mr. Sullivan hearing this, threatened me that if I should change his design in the slightest degree I would never get another piece of work from him — a pledge he kept.

In the end Mr. Temple's objections prevailed and changes were made. I believe Mr. Sullivan in the heat of argument was standing on principal, but was secretly pleased, and liked it better with the elimination of the lions and children., so it remained without any substitution.

This was not the only offence to my art. I was to be stricken with another affront. I was told that Lillian Russell, a famous beauty, and daughter of my good friend Cynthia Leonard, star of the play that was to open the theater, objected to the spandrel figure representing Diana resting her hand on a peacock. Miss Russell saw it while being shown the beautiful new theater, and she refused to perform unless the objectionable symbol of beauty, the peacock, about which many theatrical people are extremely superstitious, was removed.

Harry Vincent, a friend of mine, and one of the country's foremost scenic aritsts, was called upon to perform the surgery. He almost wept in recounting the story to me and apologized for the sacrilege which left an oddly vacant space on the panel.

It was almost a year before the opening of the World's Columbian Exposition, better known as the Chicago World's Fair. All the beautiful buildings were completed and ready for the exhibits to be put in place. The Immense Manufacturers Building, which was the world's largest building in floor space at that time, was a wonderfully impressive structure, and no doubt deserved to stand next to the gem of all the buildings, Sullivan's Transportation Building with its rainbow arch entrance. He was accorded national and international praise for its message of pure architectural tenets.

Now that the Schiller theater was completed I still had a considerable amount of work that needed attention. There was the exhibition piece I was to do for the Manufacturers' Building, the Schlitz Brewery trademark of a huge globe with a buckled belt around it. This globe was supported by four female figures in playful poses representing the four hemispheres. At their feet were gnomes. Flanking this centerpiece were four pedestals constructed of beer kegs, three to a pedestal, and on top of each a herald blowing a trumpet. This work was in charge of an assistant named Franz Rugiska with whom I had made a partnership agreement. He had come to me from Mr. Sullivan's sculptor, Mr. Boyle, who had worked on the

Schiller Theatre Spandrel including the offending peacock

Transportation Building while I was doing the Schiller Theater.

While I was doing this work I was also remodeling a barn into another studio so I could begin my Indianapolis Library group which I had been putting off due to the pressure of other work. There were some other minor pieces that needed my attention. One other large work at this same time was a panel of the Seal of Costa Rica, for which I engaged the well-known painter Charles Francis Brown. At this time he was stranded in Chicago and I helped him for quite some time, so when he left for New York he had money in his pocket and his debts were paid.

My newly remodeled studio was ready for my larger work, but I was destined to regret this studio venture for it would soon be winter and I had made no provision for suitably heating the large premises. However, I buoyantly entered upon my tasks, come what may. I passed through that first winter with considerable difficulty, freezing both my clay model and my live one.

All things finally have an end, and with the coming of spring, with the aid of my assistant, Franz Rugiska, and my pupil James Earl Frazer, the work was soon completed and cast in bronze. This group, over fifty years later, is still an impressive piece of sculpture.[6]

Rugiska stayed with me but a short time, finishing a memorial bust of John Huss, the Bohemian martyr. Hard times had set in and he decided he would do better in New York even though a serious depression was effecting the entire country.

Coxey's Army of unemployed men was on its famous march to Washington to petition Congress to take measures to relieve unemployment. The strike of the Railroad Switchmen had tied up transportation, and the times just before the Chicago Fair opened were serious. The brilliant leadership of Eugene V. Debs, president of the union avoided disaster, but trumped up charges landed him in jail, and gave me the unique opportunity to model a portrait of him, which I did in the Cook County jail in Chicago.[7]

About this time a natural disaster occured within view of my studio which was located at Lake Park Avenue and 33rd Street. Lake storms are always fearful for they usually come up with little or no warning and are of frightening ferocity. This was such a storm, striking havoc with shipping and blowing dozens of cargo ships from their moorings into tangled masses all along the shore. A ship loaded with lumber was dashed to pieces on the rocks and human beings were mangled by the floating lumber and crushed upon the outcropping rocks by the fury of the storm. A woman and a child had been tied to the cabin of a ship in a vain effort to protect them until aid could arrive, but it was unavailing and they were dashed to their deaths before the helpless people on shore.

Lake storms subside as quickly as they start, and after this storm had calmed I took a walk along the shore as far as 18th Street, and I was impressed by the great shore damage and the unusual coloration of the sky which seemed to reflect the tragedy that had just taken place.

The fury of the storm had destroyed the celebrated "Massacre Oak" which had stood at the foot of 18th Street and Prairie Avenue on the lake. Sometime later the Pullman family erected a monument by the Danish sculpotr, Karl Kohl-Smith, to mark the location.

The studio was experiencing a lull in large commissions, but I had a number of portraits to do and I was engaged in some competitions: one a very good effort for a monument of General Philip Henry Sheridan, to be erected in Lincoln Park in Chicago. It was a gift of Mr. Yerke, the street car magnate, who indulged himself in art. The competition was in the hands of a man numaed Fulton who urged me to participate, and assured me the competition was being conducted honestly. Beside myself, the contestants were Gutzon Borglum and Hermon MacNeil. Because I was anxious to make an impressive entry I hired a horse from a livery stable for a number of days as a model. Frazer took charge, riding the horse to and from the stable each day. I was well versed in animal anatomy but I always used a live model if possible. I was pleased with my entry which was consistant and had logical lines. I received considerable priase for my work, but Borglum's entry was the one chosen.

While I failed in this I was engaged in a less ambitious effort, a soldiers' monument competition at Lancaster, Pennsylvania, which I won. It was a group of figures representing two soldiers defending the flag. This monument stands on the battlefield at Chickamauga.

Model for Lancaster, Pennsylvania, Soldiers' Monument

Chapter VIII
1894-1895

The World's Columbian Exposition of 1893 had left quite a large influx of artists who decided to stay in Chicago. They were young, ambitious and progressive artists whose thoughts were at a tangent to the conservative established group respresented by those attached to the Chicago Art Institute and the Chicago Society of Artists. These newcomers, together with the more progressive local artists, organized a new society and called it The Cosmopolitan Club of Chicago.

Some of the members became nationally and internationally known in the art world, among them Arthur Dawson, Frank S. Payraud, George L. Schreiber, Roberto Raskovich, Hadesti Maratta, Harry Vincent, Harry Wallace Methven, Max Mauch, Emory Albright, Alfred Jurgens, Arthur Feuedel, James Earl Frazer, A. J. Rupert and Leon Roecker.

The first exhibition by the club was held in the Stevens Gallery of the Atheneum Building. I designed the cover for the catalogue which was generously illustrated. The exhibition was a huge success, and was destined to be a challenge to the older established artists of the city who saw their accepted prestige slipping away to the members of this new organization. And well they might be concerned, for in time the new society and its members became the leaders.

Now, as I am writing this, all is peace and quiet. All that was mortal of these friends and colleagues is gone, but the spirit of their souls and the greatness of their works live on.

This group of kindred spirits used to meet in the studios of the various members. More often than not, it was in my studio that the meetings were held as my studio was large, and I was friendly with all of them. At one time, in order to lighten the routine of our daily lives, it was decided to hold a stag party which was enthusiastically approved by all the members who gave their whole-hearted support. It was to be held in my studio.

Each member chose a particular contribution. Roberto Raskovich prepared the spaghetti. For this he used a well-scrubbed clothes boiler, and received permission from the land-lady to use the laundry stove in the basement. George Schreiber selected his favorite accomplishement of German Pancakes. Another contributed cigars and cigarettes. Others contributed a large tub of ice-cream, cold cuts, sausages and cheese with whatever accompaniments were desired.

I had recently completed a portrait for Philip Moran, one of the members of a well-known bottling concern. For pyament of the work he proposed supplying me with an adquate amount of bottled goods: various wines, liquors, cordials, and a keg of beer with a spigot to draw the beer from the keg; these were my contribution.

Loredo Taft from the Art Institute was not a member. But he was invited, and he came. He, Charles Francis Brown and Hermon MacNeil came in Indian costumes, and some of the others wore costumes to add to the festivities. The neighborhood for a block around the studio had been informed of the party, and that it might be late.

Due to the kindness of my male model, we had a congenial helper and head waiter. The party opened very sedately. The spaghetti, prepared by Raskovich, was pure Italian style with tender chicken and a superb sauce. He and my model also served as bartenders and saw to it that all glasses were continually replenished. Everyone acclaimed it a feast par excellence. A toast was proposed to the chef in a speech by one of the members, with many compliments.

In the mean time George Schreiber was struggling with his pancakes, and they were finally ready to be served. Our head waiter, wishing to make this accomplished feat a special occasion, attempted to balance a large tray full of pancakes on one hand as he carried them to the festive board. But disaster overtook him as he slipped on some beer that had been spilled on the floor, and the tray flew into the air cascading a shower of pancakes all over the guests. Nothing daunted, they entered into the spirit of the evening, and the second serving of the pancakes were declared delicious. But poor George, disappointed and chagrined after all his effort, sought solace in a big glass of beer.

The dinner was about over, the ice cream had been consumed and black coffee served. Finally a calm set in as after a storm, and the party began to break up, with everyone agreeing it had been a perfect success amid promises to repeat it in the future.

A group who lived in the same direction as myself were waiting for a street car at about three in the morning. Harry Vincent, who was a big chap, about six feet, three inches, was feeling in a talkative mood, loudly expostulating about something. The policeman on the beat remonstrated with him about the propriety of making a disturbance at such an early hour. Harry did not agree with this and he proceeded to lecture the policeman on the rights of the individual and freedom of speech in the United States. Fortunately this partiuclar arm of the law was very understanding and had a sense of humor, but what really saved the situation was the arrival of our street car.

The next morning, at about ten o'clock when Frazer and I arrived at the studio we found our friend Schreiber sound asleep on a couch, and very difficult to arouse. He declared up and down that he had not been intoxicated. It was true he had been unable to get home when we left for he lived in Washington Heights and there was no transportation at that time of night.

The task of converting the banquet hall back to the functions of a studio was finally completed, and life settled back to the regular routine.

One of my next works was the Lovejoy Monument, erected in Alton, Illinois. It consisted of a bronze Winged Victory, two tripods and two eagles, all mounted on supporting columns.

The first procedure for a large statue is to make a working model half or quarter size of the permanent statue. A pointing machine is constructed in order to enlarge the small model to one of full size. An open box-like frame is built which houses the model. This frame is ruled off into equal numbered spaces with corresponding sides similarly marked off. A ruled bar containing an adjustable ruled stylus completes the arrangement. This bar is clamped in various positons on the framework while the stylus gives the depth within the space at any point it comes in contact with the model. A similar framework is constructed of a proportional size to that desired for the finished statue, with proportionally enlarged marking on the framework. Then the horizontal bar and stylus are put in their proper positions. The stylus will mark a point of proportional depth with the large framework that the smaller stylus marks upon the model. This is the method used in enlarging or diminishing an original model.

The large model has an armature or supporting framework and on this the form is built up entirely of plaster, its form being determined by the proportional points determined by the stylus.

The small model, modeled in clay, then cast in plaster, is finished down to the minutest detail so no irregularities will appear in the enlarged statue. After the statue in the enlargement has been completed in plaster, it is then cast in bronze.

Lovejoy Monument

Bronze casting is a very complicated procedure, and I will quote the climax of the process from the section on bronze casting in my book "The Techniques of Sculpture."

"It is an exciting spectacle and a tense moment when a big volume of metal is poured, and it is always accompanied by shouts from the Boss to 'Hurry up' and 'Easy now.' The crucibles are set aside, and everyone stands far enough away so as not to be hit by any of the sputtering metal. The Boss steps up quickly to the furnace, his face and hands shielded, and as he pulls out the plug you hear the bubbling, gurgling and sputtering of the metal inside the mold. You might say she boils and blows like a whale. Everyone stays at a distance as though expecting the thing to explode, and in the din, giving voice to this tense, dramatic moment, the voice of Mr. Bercham, the French Boss, carried above every other sound, in a polyglot of English, ordering the men about to such endearing names as Horse or Gorilla. The Boss also steps out of harm's way but like a real general, he is on the firing line watching every move.

"As the metal reaches the top of the mold, the newspapers which were stuck in the openings catch fire, igniting the escaping gasses, shooting out varicolored flames, and as the metal comes to the top it flows over into small basins of sand formed around the vents.

"The Boss draws a long breath and becomes suddenly congenial, 'Allez - done,' he says, and takes me into his small office. 'Que connais tu?' and he brings out a bottle of wine. 'A votre sante.'

"When the metal has had time to cool, the fastenings and the boards around the mold are opened, the hard sand dug out, and the bronze replica of the sculptor's brain-child sees the light of day. From there much work lies ahead before completion."

Several years had elapsed since the Schiller Theater Building when I met Anton Hessing. One day I received a note from Mrs. Werkmeister, asking me to help her decorate her home for the birthday celebration for my good friend Hessing. I was very happy to have the opportunity to do this, and when I outlined my idea to the family, they were delighted. My main feature was the working model of my Winged Victory figure which was four feet high. I mounted it on a table in an alcove window surrounded by banked potted plants and ferns and palms. The party was a delightful affair and Mr. Hessing was pleased with my contribution.

Mrs. Werkmeister and her husband, who was a druggist, had a large house, and Mr. Hessing made his home with them.

Sometime later Mr. Hessing and Mrs. Werkmeister collaborated in establishing the German Old People's Home. In Waldheim Cemetery there are two bronze tablets in bas relief, one by Carl Mauch of Mrs. Werkmeister, and the other by me of Mr. Hessing.

Frazer, who was still with me, and I used to box for exercise and relaxation. We derived a great deal of pleasure from our sparring, and I learned a lot from him for he was an expert. Mrs. Werkmeister's son Arthur, a hospital intern, was a frequent visitor at the studio and he kept reiterating what wonderful boxers some of the fellows at the hospital were, and was continually after us to agree to a match.

Finally we agreed. The event took place at the hospital. My first

Martha Methven, Richard W. Bock
Harry Wallace Methven — c. 1895

opponent was a boxer with a razzle-dazzle technique I could not overcome and I was at his mercy. Next, I boxed with a very tall chap who had me at a distinct disadvantage because of his much longer reach. Once again I went down to defeat. Frazer now took each of them on in order to pay them back for my defeat. He was a very hard hitter and he was able to hit them at will while neither was able to lay a glove on him. Afterward we had a very pleasant meal and really enjoyed ourselves.

My studio was a favorite rendezvous where plans were developed for the Cosmpolitan Art Club by those who were most active. I had become very friendly with one of the members, Harry Wallace Methven, a very talented and promising artist. He frequently invited me to his home, and occasionally to tea. There were seven children in this family, five boys and two girls, and the widowed mother. She was a very proud, patrician lady, descended from distinguished early American lineage which was clearly reflected in the handsome children. The father, a Civil War veteran, had died a number of years before.

Again, I was smitten by cupid's arrow, coming from the youngest and fairest member of this interesting family. From all indications this was a non-marrying family as only the oldest son was married, and to a cousin. It would require some strategy to overcome the barriers and vigilance that surrounded my princess. I knew I had to rescue her from her loving family. I found a way to breach this stronghold where they seemed to be perfectly content with themselves and wanted no intruders. At this time I was working on my Winged victory and I needed someone to pose for the head. When my friend Harry Methven came to see me, I very discreetly suggested my idea of having his beautifiul sister Martha pose for it. He seemed agreeable and a date was set. She came, and now I could feast my eyes upon this charming, lovely maiden to my heart's content, though her distance only made her the more desirable. I longed to explore the hidden depths of her emotions which her lovely face betrayed. We were able to have enough conversation to become acquainted, which was impossible at her home with so many watchful eyes.

After waiting a few days I made my next move. I wrote a note asking for the pleasure of her company to a theater performance, say the Schiller Theater. If agreeable I would appreciate a reply. Again I availed myself of her artist brother Harry to be cupid's messenger to his lovely sister. In a few days I had a favorable reply to my note. She fixed the date, and when I called I obtained the mother's consent. As for the theater performance, it was lost to me in the pleasure of having Martha sitting at my side. Going home was not by ordinary conveyance, I was floating on air. Arriving at her home and back to earth at the same time, we tarried in the vestibule to make another date to meet. The answer came with but a single kiss and quick-as-a-hare "good night," as she darted out of reach. I went on my way, again floating on air, as I relived the pleasure of the evening and the strange magic of that single kiss. It seemed tangible, I could feel it like something real. It was like a token from heaven for I can still remember it felt heavenly. It was all mine, and a million dollars would not have taken it from me. There it was, attached to my face like a magnificant jewel set there upon my burning cheek, and I was proud of it.

Frazer, too, expressed himself in ravishing terms about Martha's beauty. Such a mouth, such lips, a masterpiece of nature. It could happen only one time in a million. Art nor artifice could enhance them. She weighed a scant one hundred pounds, her height five feet six inches, her complexion a brunette with large brown eyes. That was Martha Methven, who later became my wife.

Frazer completed two study heads, one was an order that would take him to Paris for a year. First, however, he entered a class at the Chicago Art Institute and won first prize in portrait drawing during his first semester. He soon left for New York. He was a very good pupil and I would miss him for we had become very close friends.

Fortune favored his career as there was a competition for designing a medal while he was in Paris. Augustus St. Gaudens was in Paris at the time and was asked to judge the competition. He gave Frazer first choice and then engaged him to work for him.

Frazer became one of our finest sculptors with many splendid public works to his credit, including the famous equestrian Indian figure "End of the Trail." He married Laura Gardin, a lovely lady who was also a sculptor, well-known for the many medals she designed.

One of my closest friends was Roberto Raskovich. He was an excellent watercolor artist and etcher. He was an interesting, romantic fellow, born in Dalmatia. In order to evade the Austrian Army draft, he went to Italy to live and study. There in Venice sat our Romeo, painting and waiting for the rich American tourists to whom he sold his paintings. With his good looks he had no difficulty. He met a pretty American girl who was touring Italy with her parents. Impulsive infatuation, and then they married and lived in Tacoma, Washington, with her parents. Cold facts made romance fly out the window, for the parents did not approve of him, and Raskovich suffered from the restraint of married life and the monotony of living in a small city. So he left his wife and moved to Chicago. Mrs. Raskovich came on to try for a reconciliation and stayed for a few weeks. I saw her quite often, and she even gave a surprise party for me. I found her very charming and willing to do anything to set matters right between them but, to make the situation impossible, Roberto had developed a deep infatuation for a strikingly beautiful blond-haired married woman. As for poor Mrs. Raskovich, her trip was useless. I went to the station with them, carrying the luggage and to say a last good-bye. They never met again. She got one prize from her marriage, a very handsome and bright son who was named Roberto after his father.

Following this unhappy parting, Raskovich and I started preparing the organization for an Artist's Festival, the first ever to be held by the Chicago Art Institute. The idea took like wildfire.

I was well acquainted with several Austrian artists who had told me about the greatest festival ever staged in Vienna. It was planned and directed by that genius Hans Makhart, the greatest decorative artist of his time. In his Festival parade he rode at the head of the column on a snow white stallion loaned for the occasion by the Royal stables. He was a very handsome man with jet black hair and finely trimmed beard, and he wore an all black riding habit. The theme of the festival was

Civilization through the Ages. The pageant was made up of floats and groups of people in costume. I have seen pictures of this pageant which must have been indescribably beautiful.

Our pageant was not so elaborate. It was mostly indoors, although we did parade about the outside of the Art Institute for a time. Then going inside the museum, the Director W. M. R. French, made an address of welcome, tendering the freedom of the galleries. Later refreshments were served in Blackstone Hall.

Students of the Art School interpreted Greek and Early American history. The Austrian group interpreted European history with Columbus and some of his crew, also Faust, Mephisto, Margaret (interpreted by Martha Methven), Rembrandt, Beethoven and others famous in history and the arts.

I was the Pied Piper of Hamlin. The costume I wore was the one worn by the well-known singer Hubert Wilke in his stage role.[8]

Roberto Raskovich's group was the most elegant of all. Composed of four people representing an Italian Duke and Duchess with two pages attending them. The pages carried silver trumpets, and the Duchess was Raskovich's blonde friend. About a dozen singers in costumes of the same 16th Century period accompanied them.

There was a group of young girls who gave a performance in rhythmic dancing. Another feature was singers from the Germania Maener Choir, who sang parts of Wagner's "Die Meistersinger."

The great hall with its replicas of medieval masterpieces of architectural sculpture made a beautiful and impressive setting for the pageant. The music, singing, dancing and comraderie made it a glorious success, and everyone expressed the hope it would be an annual event.

The pageant was repeated a number of times in the following years, but only by the students in the school.

Self Portrait, as Pied Piper of Hamlin

Chapter IX
1896-1898

Early in March of 1896 I received a letter from the architect Dwight Heald Perkins asking me to call at his office in the Steinway Building in regard to some work. When I arrived he explained that it was for the Trans-Mississippi Exposition in Omaha which was then in the course of construction. He had the commission for the Machinery and Electricity building on which he had included some large sculpture. It was comprised of four groups at the corners of the building, and a tower-like elevation at the center of the building. The whole was to represent "Man's Struggle for Control of Nature's Forces."

The first requisite was to make preliminary sketches of the whole project. This work had to be handled with the utmost speed for the sketches and models had to be approved by the Governing Board of Architects for the Exposition, consisting of Howard Walker and Thomas R. Kimball, before work could be started on the ten foot high groups which had to be finished and in place by early fall.

I completed the sketches to the satisfaction of Mr. Perkins, but it was necessary for me to take them to Omaha for inspection and approval by the Board. I left without delay and they were accepted without change by the Board. The trip was not without incident, for on my return to Chicago I decided to stop off in Ft. Dodge, Iowa, to make a quick call upon my sister who was married and living there.

To get there from Omaha necessitated changing trains at a small crossing station. I was obliged to cross a vacant piece of ground of about a quarter mile in order to get from one train to the other. The train I was to take was already waiting for passengers, but I was the only one making the change, and as it was midnight the conductor was unable to see me. I was running and shouting to him but he did not hear me. Being heavily burdened with my gear, even though I exerted myself to the utmost, I barely reached the last car of the train as it started to move. I tossed my luggage on to the steps of the moving train and with supreme effort was just able to grasp hold and climb aboard. It was bitter cold standing on the bare open platform without any protection, and the constant swaying and jerking of the fast-moving train threatened to dislodge me even though I was holding on for dear life. As the door into the car was locked, and all my efforts to open it or make someone hear me were useless, I was obliged to remain in my precarious position until the next time the train stopped at a station, which seemed to take hours.

When the train finally stopped, the conductor was very surprised to see me and wanted to know where I had come from. But my agony was over and I continued my journey in comfort and warmth. I reached Ft. Dodge early the next morning, stayed for a day and a very pleasant visit with my sister, then back to Chicago where I immediately started the formidable work on the Exposition groups.

Model of central group, Mining and Electricity Building. Trans-Mississippi Exposition, Omaha

First I had to make the working clay models which required finding suitable male models. I was fortunate, for I found a man over six feet tall and weighing over two hundred pounds. He was an exhibition strong man who entertained his audience by driving spikes through one inch boards with his bare hands, easily breaking chains tied around his chest, and many other similar feats. But strong as this giant was he was unable to hold a pose longer than five minutes at a time. He perspired profusely and twitched all over because his muscles were so over-developed.

The statuary for the building included one group showing a strong man strangling a lion reared up on its hind legs, and another man who had fallen to the ground. The second group included a man standing with one foot on a prostrate lion, with spear and shield protecting a woman and a small child with a dog on one side looking down at the lion. These two groups were duplicated, making four groups. The center group showed man triumphant, standing in a chariot, driving a span of five lions. A figure stood on each side holding an emblem, one of machinery, the other of electricity. A model of an eagle, reproduced four times was part of the four supporting columns.

The one-fourth scale working models were modeled in clay, then cast in plaster. Then they all had to be modeled in clay again in their finished size, with the figures about ten feet tall. I had to finish the working models in less than five weeks and take them to Omaha where the finished works had to be in place by the first of November. Against that herculean task I had youth, strength, ability, an abiding confidence, a blissful ignorance of the indeterminable, and a stake in love as an incentive. I also gambled with luck.

I succeeded in assembling the assistants I would need. There were two women who had been students at the Art Institute: a Miss Monroe and a Miss Cooper, Ed Sawyer, Martha Methven's twin brother Huston, a dental student on his summer vacation, and Jack Bauer, a boy of sixteen I thought would be useful for running errands. Also Theador Lau, a master plaster caster.

This little group arrived in Omaha with all our preparations and plans completed so we could begin work immediately.

It was now the first of May, 1897, and our first act on arrival was to find a place to live and a studio in which to work. We might just as well have been cast up on the shore of a desert isle. We had no shelter, nor any friends in this city, neither did we have any money. All of my efforts had been on completion of the models and making preparations for uninterrupted work in Omaha, and I had not given a thought to arranging funds to see us through. The organization in charge of the Exposition made no arrangements and were of no assistance to us. However, our immediate problem was solved by the generosity of faithful Sawyer who turned over the three hundred dollars he had brought with him. He also was the one who found a workshop, a boarding house, and a good restaurant, all within a radius of about a block of each other, and all within a few hours of our arrival. This was accomplished through the help of a Mr. Stoddard, who solved all our problems. He had just completed a house with a number of bedrooms in preparation for the host of visitors expected to attend the Exposition. This building took care of our shelter. Across the street was a family who served our meals. The workshop was also on Mr. Stoddard's property. It was a long barn, and he even put up a lean-to at one end for use as a plaster-casting room, and this workshop was not far from the Exposition grounds. Our first day in Omaha had been a fruitful one; our luck had held out, and we needed very bit of it.

Mr. Stoddard was a lanky, typical farmer type, who had lost an eye in an accident, but it was generally believed he had lost it in a war, a belief he did not take the trouble to correct. He had recently returned from a successful sheep drive. He drove 25,000 head of sheep to the stock yards, foraging them on government grazing land. This feat was widely publicised, and there were many who tried to imitate him but without success. His wife was a small, lean woman, good natured but exact, and it was she who held the purse strings. Fortunately, they were both well satisfied with our group.

The day after our arrival we were greeted by a benevolent sun with a warm and cheery welcome, so we took a rest after our strenuous first day getting settled. The next day our activities really started. The first

Burlington Station, Omaha, Nebraska

thing was to procure materials. Consulting my right-hand man, Ed Sawyer, we ordered a ton of potter's clay, lumber, iron pipes and a ton of molding plaster. The two girls went to the Exposition grounds where they saw what progress was being made on the buildings.

The preliminary preparations for our work consisted mainly in building armatures. These were constructed directly upon the dirt floor of our studio by driving two six inch square, eight foot posts into the ground about six feet apart, leaving about five feet of the posts extending above ground. Horizonatally, atop these posts, I secured an iron pipe with a "T" joint in the center. This structure was to support the standing figure for which I had developed a novel, adjustable skeleton made of iron pipes with adjustable joints, so it could be used for all the other figures as well, each being modeled and cast in succession. It was an original idea and worked very successfully, saving a great deal of time.

The other objects, the eagle, lion and dog were the first to be completed because they required four replicas of one original, except the dog which required only two. This permitted our plaster caster to keep busy while we progressed with the other work. All of these molds were piece molds because of the need for duplication. All of the work proceeded with speed and efficiency. Miss Monroe modeled the reclining figure, and Miss Cooper, the woman and child.

Huge quantities of materials were used, and Mr. Lau was extremely resourceful in utilizing materials readily available, or in being able to find substitutes. Forty tons of plaster and buckets of lard-oil were used in the casting.

We also did our own foraging, buying a small second-hand stove, and using a length of six-inch pipe that we found on the property as an anvil.

The weather was beautiful and continued in our favor for which we were very grateful. However, it did occasionally rain, and the rain was usually a downpour which lasted only a few minutes. Our barn stood in the center of a declivity, so each time it rained we found ourselves in a minor flood, and generally had to seek temporary shelter on higher ground.

These sudden little squalls usually offered a slight diversion, for on the property was a ewe who, like Mr. Stoddard, was blind in one eye. When it rained she and her baby got very excited. Huston Methven, who was a lover of animals, would attempt to rescue them in order to get the baby out of the rain. They were very skittish and would shy away from him as he sloshed around in the water and mud which was over ankle deep. He found the only way he could make any progress was to approach the ewe on her blind side, but by the time he managed to get them to shelter it had usually stopped raining, but we had had a little respite from our labors.

We were making good progress, and each day followed the same routine of work, with eating and sleeping as minor interruptions. I had one disappointment. Jack Bauer, the sixteen year old boy became so homesick I had to send him home.

Sunday was observed as a day of rest, when we all went our own way. Sawyer and the girls had discovered a huge buffalo in an enclosure, and they made a clay model of it. Huston, on the other hand, had also discovered something: a large restaurant where he met a fellow who was a song plugger and had the concession for some of the entertainment for the Exposition. He was already doing business and offered Huston a job if he could sing. He tried out and was immediately hired. He had a loud, pleasant voice and was very good-looking like his twin sister, Martha. He was an instant hit with the ladies which made it necessary for me to keep a watch over him as I was responsible to his family. The song he had to sing innumerable times a day went partly like this:

"Your key don't fit this lock,
You best go 'round the block.
You broke your faith with me,
You no more will I see . . . " etc.

He was having a wonderful time, and did not seem to mind the lyrics.

I had my oil paints with me and went out sketching along the bluffs above the Missouri River, north of the city limits where the city water works were located, and where there were picturesque fishermen's boats. Our master plaster caster had already located some Danish friends and enjoyed a few glasses of beer with them. Everyone relaxed and enjoyed themselves, then usually congregated at our boarding house for dinner, refreshed and able to withstand the rigors of work the next week would bring. Sunday was also the day to catch up on letter writing.

There were a number of other sculptors who had commissions. One in particular, a good friend whose artistic ability I admired, was Emile Wuertz. He had but a single figure to do, of Neptune, God of the Sea. It stood upon a column at one end of a long lagoon, overlookig Venetian gondolas and their passengers. Emile had been unfortunate in his life, and this commission was a godsend. His heroic statue of Neptune was splendidly done, and the money he received would take him back to Paris. Alas, fate had planned it otherwise. The French liner upon which he travelled collided with an iceberg, and nearly all the passengers perished, including Emile whose body was found in the crowded hold of the ship. With him was a young lady with his coat around her, silently indicating another romance. He was a true and noble artist, and the world was made poorer by his loss. His statue of Neptune was a fitting memorial to him.

I have already described one enlarging device, when maximum accuracy is required. In the present case we used another method of enlarging, while not as accurate suffices for most ordinary work. This is done by proportional dividers, an instrument called a caliper, which consists of two straight or slightly curved arms with pin pointers at each end, and fastened by a movable axis where they cross to form an X. The space separating the pointers at each end is always proportional, so that when the degree of enlarging or diminishing has been decided upon, and the movable axis has been fastened in its proper place by a screw, all reference points on the large figure can be checked with the corresponding points on the small model.

In the present group of models, effect was most important. They must be bold and have an interesting contour. The theme of the work necessitated a bold treatment with no fine or small detail for the character of the subject would be lost at the distance they were to be seen.

A number of weeks had passed since we first started our work in Omaha, a great deal of progress had been made, and my fellow workers needed a bit of fun and relaxation. So a few days before my birthday, which is on July 16, I decided to have a birthday party. For dinner we had chicken, wine, ice cream and a big birthday cake as well as a box of fudge my sweetheart had made and sent to me. There was sufficient not only for us, but for all the people at whose house we boarded, who had complained a number of times that with our young and healthy appetites we were eating them out of house and home.

Songs were part of the festivities, and after "Happy Birthday" and other favorites, they put a new ending on an old doggerel:

"For He's a Jolly Good Fellow,
For He's a Jolly Good Fellow,
For He's a Jolly Good Fellow
When he gets a letter from home."

I had heard it rumored that I was grumpy and hard to get along with if I didn't get a letter from Martha. My thirty-second birthday passed very pleasantly and everyone had a good time.

We were now ready to erect the central platform carrying the main group. This required an extra-strong structure to support it against the elements. There was a carpenter on the site who specialized in this character of work and had worked on the Chicago World's Fair in 1893.

The lions and eagles were completed and the standard bearers were ready for casting, two reproductions from one model. The standing figure with spear and shield protecting a mother and child were being modeled, and soon would be duplicated in plaster. This left but two figures to be modeled, one standing in the chariot, and the other, the lion tamer. The figure on the ground in this group was already in plaster. The end of August would see all of the clay models completed and the erecting of the groups in progress. Lions, chariot and eagles were in place, and we could see how good my judgement had been for effect.

Thomas Kimball, the architect, came in only once to inspect the work. There could be no doubt that everything was satisfactory and that he was pleased, for he offered me a much bigger and better commission, to do the pediments for the new Chicago, Burlington and Quincy Railroad Station in Omaha. The commission was to have gone to Daniel Chester French, the famous sculptor and creator of many outstanding masterpieces. That instead he had given it to me was a great compliment. The commission would keep me in Omaha a year longer, which put the ringing of wedding bells in jeopardy and called for an explanation. That problem was solved, but not without some regret, and I soon went back to work.

By the end of August there was no more work for the girls. I surmise they left with no regrets, being able to live a more normal life again after a summer of hard work. For our part they had been a fine morale stabilizer, as in the case of Mr. Lau, the plaster caster who would vent chagrin and anger with a long "Cheeeeee," and when asked what it meant, said it meant "Jesus Christ," but he didn't want to come right out and say it before the ladies. He was a splendid caster, and when he was through with my work, the Chicago Art Institute engaged him and he was there for many years. Years later, during Prohibiton, he was so angry at not being able to get his daily beer, he went back to Denmark, but did not stay long, and returned to Chicago.

The work was all completed by the end of September, leaving ample time for spray-painting to protect the work from the hard winter weather. Our effort had created an effect that was strikingly bold and I was pleased that it was a fine achievement. It always seems too bad that none of these works are ever made in permanent material, but are always destroyed at the end of the Exposition or Fair.

I was staying on, but Huston Methven, like a star that had been born and gloried in his short-lived popularity as a singer, had to return to Chicago to matriculate at Northwestern University Dental School on the first of October. He would have liked to stay on, but he was my responsibility, and I was on trial by my sweetheart's family. I am glad to report he became an eminent dentist in Chicago.

The Stoddards remained my friends to the end of my sojourn in Omaha. He had been of tremendous help in all we did. He had found me an ideal studio at a reasonable rental and it was satisfactory for my purpose. It was a small hall, 25 by 65 feet, on the third floor of the building. It had a row of windows along one side and a hallway on the opposite side with a door that opened toward the alley. This door had a projecting beam overhead upon which a pulley could be fastened in order to lift heavy objects from the alley below. It had an adjoining small room which I used for sleeping quarters. My studio had electric light, steam heat and elevator service. The building was conveniently located in the heart of the city, next door to the post office, and was largely occupied by the Sherman Wholesale Chemical Company. Directly across the street was a good restaurant where I had most of my meals, and one block away was the architect's office. I could hardly ask for anything better.

I made my models of the pediments one-half size, which meant the figures stood five feet high. They were framed in the familiar style of classic cornices. I had these cornices done for me while I concentrated on the figure work.

The modeling required a large platform and a blackboard upon which the clay was modeled. These working models were for the use of the stone carvers who would make the full-size groups. The carving was done by Evans and Coombs of Boston. The man in charge of the work was named Statler, and he had several men under him.

First, was the preliminary task of making the small sketch models which entailed developing the design and composition, and upon which the architect would pass. In this case, Howard Walker, Tom Kimball's associate architect, passed on my work. He had a suggestion, and to clarify his criticism, he made a small working drawing which was a definite aid to me as it was very well done.

I was soon well established with all of the necessities, and the work was progressing nicely. But alas, one morning I was awakened by loud voices in the hallway and the smell of smoke in the air. Sitting up, I heard the chug of an engine in the street and then someone pounding on my door. I dressed in a hurry, and grabbing my overcoat I joined the throng in the street. The fire had started in the Chemical Company quarters, and did little damage as it was soon under control.

One day Tom Kimball came to see me and brought Lorado Taft from the Chicago Art Institute to show him my work. He complimented me highly and called it a "Phidias performance."

The modeling of the pediment was nearly completed and ready for casting. It was the month of April, 1899, and again I had need of my friend Stoddard to find another studio for me because some of the tenants of the building failed to appreciate an artist at work, and objected to the mess created by my clay and plaster, so I had to relinquish these ideal quarters.

Mr. Stoddard often came to see me, and it was always at a most opportune time. This time I was delighted to see him, and stated my problem. Kind and resourceful as he was, he was able to find suitable accommodations for me, although they were in a different section of the city. This time it was an empty store and it suited my purpose quite well. The interruption of moving affected my timing for only one day, and I had enough lumber, fiber, clay and plaster to finish the entire job. If my friend Stoddard had not provided me with a perfectly satisfactory place to live and work everything would have been much more difficult for me. As it was, this change was rather desirable for I had an excellent room and some good home cooking. My landlady was a former school teacher whose husband was a travelling salesman selling lightening rods. My new living quarters were just a pleasant walk from my studio workshop, and as it was the month of May, there were flowers and birds and little children playing along the way. It was truly very pleasant.

I completed the modeling of the large pediment which measured eighty-one feet horizontally from tip to tip; the center height sixteen feet and the depth of the relief carving was sixteen inches. In the center, mounted on a base, was a clock set in a wreath of oak leaves.

There were ten figures in all, standing on either side of the center wreath, representing Steam and Electricity. Two more standing figures represented Mercury (for travel) and Finance. There were two seated female figures on each side. They represented Agriculture, Manufacture, Art and Literature. A reclining figure was on each end.

After the modeling was completed, the whole was cast in plaster. I had already purchased a ton of plaster and secured the services of a caster who did quite a satisfactory job. The molds being completed, I found it impractical to produce the positive from molds of such size, so they had to be made in pieces of a size that could be handled. As it was, some of the pieces weighed from two to three hundred pounds. Again, friend Stoddard found the right kind of moving outfit. A flat-top dray and horse with all the necessary equipment necessary to lift and lower the sections by pulley onto the dray. The projecting beam to which the pulley was attached gave me some qualms, and the Italian caster was in mortal fear of it and would not go near, but sought a safe place out of harm's way. It took two full loads to move it without incident.

I was informed that the stone-carver and his men from Boston would soon arrive. They would be busy for at least a week putting up scaffolding which would give me ample time to complete the positive cast from the mold. This would be a waste mold which means that after the plaster has been poured making the positive cast, the mold is chipped away and destroyed in the process. Only one cast is possible from such a mold.

I had the second pediment to create which was smaller than the first. This would be placed in the gabled field of the portico of the station, supported by a double row of polished granite columns. This pediment had a clock framed in a laurel wreath in the center and a figure on each side. One represented a woman with a greyhound at her feet, and the other an Indian woman with her papoose with the head and hide of a buffalo at her feet.

With this pediment I had no time limit because the carving of the large pediment would take some time and I had to stay until they had completed both pediments for my contract stipulated that I would oversee the installation and put the finishing touches on the carving.

I had all summer to complete this one pediment. Of course I did not intend to tarry on the job but I was not rushed and did not need any assistance. It gave me time for some much needed rest and recreation, and I often visited my friend Stoddard who was an interesting character.

One time he took me in a horse-driven buckboard to one of his farms where I saw corn growing nine feet high, and other crops which grew equally well in the terrific heat of the Nebraska sun. As we travelled along he would pass the time by telling stories which always demonstrated his cleverness and great sagacity. He would often dwell upon the blindness of one eye, and be amused at the advantage it gave him, for people did not know which eye was blind and it confused them.

I had one more request of him: to find a greyhound for me to use as a model, and even that he succeeded in doing. I did not intend to leave all of his kindness to go unrewarded, so I suggested I would make a portrait bust of him, which pleased him very much. We discussed the blind, eyeless socket, and he thought as I did that it should be indicated, but when he came for further posing he brought the final verdict from Mrs. Stoddard. She wanted it made so he had two good eyes so she might enjoy her spouse's appearance as God had intend him to be.

I had one other friend in Omaha, Laurie Wallace, a painter I had met in Chicago years before when the Trilby and Svengali craze was at its height. He was called Svengali for he was the image of the character as represented in drawings and in the theater. We saw each other occassionally, and he was very helpful in securing models for me. But mostly I applied myself to completion of the last pediment, and spent my Sundays painting in the country. I made about twenty sketches that summer.

The stone carvers were making fine headway and would soon require the last of the models. The entire job was completed in good time, and I spent many days working with the men and putting the final finishing touches on the carvings.

I was very pleased with the result, and contemplated with satisfaction and some pride the work which would be a landmark for the city of Omaha.

So, finally everything was completed and I could return home to my patiently waiting sweetheart.

But I also had a disappointment. If you happen to be in Omaha you will look in vain to find that which I have described. Years later, when I was in Omaha between trains, I was surprised to see the station had been completely remodeled, and four blank walls ten stories high, devoid of any vestige of art stood on the site. This desecration was not brought about by fire or disaster, but for practical purposes only, without regard for aesthetics.

I try to find consolation in the hope that this art work, so carefully evolved, has not been destroyed, but may find a resting place in a museum or a park, or perchance if discarded, is buried deep in the ground somewhere where future archaeologists will discover it as something from the past.

The year 1897 is an especially memorable one for me for it marked the beginning of my odyssey of working with Frank Lloyd Wright, which was to last until he left his family and went in another direction; but our close and enduring friendship never faltered.

Though our characters and dispositions were entirely different, we found much to admire in each other and always enjoyed being together.

The finger of our destinies pointed to the same road, and our collaborations were always successful.

Our working association began in the Steinway Hall Building where a group of similar souls in architecture had built their respective nests. Among them were Wright, who was always the dominant character wherever he was; Dwight Heald Perkins, who had been the architect for the Steinway Hall Building and had leased the loft on the upper floor, and then sublet it to the other aspiring young architects including Myron Hunt, who I recall, soon left for California; Arthur Huen, a very attractive personality; Robert Spencer, an artistic chap, soaring in the clouds; Tomlins, who had the misfortune of working with Wright and being unhappy and grumbling about him to me; and a draughtsman named Probst who was working with Perkins, and later became a well-known architect.

Wright asked me to do a small job of a panel for a house he was doing for a Mrs. Heller. This panel was a repetitive portion of a frieze running all the way around the building. Wright was still strongly influenced by Sullivan for it was a totally sullivanesque pattern. As an inducement to do the freize he asked me to model a portrait statue of his son John, which was intended for the children's playroom in the home he was building in Oak Park. The figure was about two feet tall and was to represent a goldenrod. John Wright was then about four years old and the most contentious model I have ever encountered. It took the combined efforts of his grandmother, Mrs. Tobin, and his older brother Lloyd, who was seven, to keep him in line so I could proceed with the statue. It eventually turned out to be an attractive piece of sculpture of a very angelic child.

In 1898 Wright moved to a new location, the Edward C. Waller building, The Rookery, where he found a new patron, and was employed as an expert consultant for the Luxfer Glass Company. This was the result of a $5,000 competition for architects, to show the way in which prism glass could be utilized as a building material.

Wright proposed to take me under his wing so I could also have a studio in The Rookery Building, first getting permission from Mr. Waller. On the top floor of the building was an all-glass room next to the light well. The room was about 50 by 50 feet and admirably suited to be a studio. The first work I did in the new studio was the pilasters for the entrance to Wright's Oak Park studio, showing storks standing among foliage beside a scroll with an architectural plan. While I was working on this he had another idea. Atop the projecting pier alongside the entrance to the studio he wanted a solid, crouching figure of a man as a terminal. For this I made a sketch representing a boulder, and I versified it with this line: "Old and strong, depressed and dreaming of an epoch past and gone." He was delighted and wanted to see it immediately, in full size. As luck would have it, I found a model for the difficult and neck-breaking position I had designed. His name was Clap, and I opened a new vocation for him, for he became one of the most outstanding models at the Chicago Art Institute.

The modeling of the figure presented an amusing incident. Nothing could go on unless Frank had his finger in the pie, so what had been laboriously completed with the model wrenching every bone and muscle

John Lloyd Wright as a Goldenrod, on a Wright Chair at the Studio entrance

"The Boulder"

in his body, Wright would come along and want to change. This made me very impatient, so I finally locked all the doors to my studio and thus prevented him from coming in. Pacing up and down in the hall outside he threatened to break in, but I paid no attention and completed the figure as I had originally designed it, and he was perfectly pleased. Some time later the art editor of the Chicago Daily News, seeing this statue on exhibition at the Art Institute proclaimed there was "a new Rodin in our midst."

But we had another crisis. Waller found out we had "a naked man up there" and even though he wore a breach-clout, from the standpoint of Mr. Waller's ethics, this did not prevent him from being a demoralizing influence upon the rest of the tenants though they never saw him. All of this resulted in a terse order to get out, bag and baggage. The Luxfer Prisim Glass Competition came to a conclusion at the same time, awarding Robert Spencer the first prize of $3,000.

Chapter X
1899

"Sarah Ann Methven wishes to announce the marriage of her daughter, Martha Higgins Methven to Richard Walter Bock, November First, Eighteen ninety-nine."

The ceremony was performed by the Reverend Mr. Lord at the Methven home on Prairie Avenue in Chicago. The bride was dressed in a beautiful white satin gown. The groom, as might be expected, was garbed in customary confusion. One thing about the day I will never forget, was the beastly weather which we received as a gift from Boreas. It had been raining, with a cold wind off the lake, and then to top it off, the rain turned to snow. But after the ceremony and reception, the night sky was clear and beautiful for the journey to the hotel where we were to spend the night.

The Reverend and Mrs. Lord were friends of the family, and they gave us a wedding gift of the use of their summer home in Benton Harbor, Michigan, for two weeks. The house was near the shore of Lake Michigan, and was completely and comfortably furnished, and even included a horse and buggy. A neighboring farmer supplied us with fresh milk, eggs and butter, and we drove Old Dobbin into town for other supplies.

It was a perfect honeymoon cottage, and the success and happiness of those first days were a forerunner of married life which included many tests and trials to prove our marriage vows were binding and worth observing.

The weather during our stay in Benton Harbor was remarkably pleasant. I was able to do some sketching with my paints, and we took long walks along the shore. We had several occasions to hitch up Dobbin to the buggy and drive to town, but the hitching up of the horse was my undoing, and my Best Half showed her superiority. She grew up with a family of boys and had spent summers on a farm.

When our stay was over we made contact with our hosts and returned their possessions with a great debt of gratitude for their gift. So we were in Chicago and facing the realistic world. First we had to find a place to live and furnish it. This occupied us for some time, and made our accumulted horde of wealth melt away like the snow under a summer sun, and necessitated me doing some "pot boilers" for immediate funds. A number came my way, and one in particular, though poor in remuneration was an amusing experience.

I received a commission from one of the ornamental decorating concerns which are noted the country over for their abortive statuary, generally done by their shop modeler. In my case, something better had been demanded. This work was for a new addition to Olson's Department Store, a leading store in Minneapolis, Minnesota.

I thought it might be a pleasant interlude, and I took my bride with me. I was full of confidence after having had so many recent successes, and felt I would finish this little task very quickly. Always full of hope and promise of a new experience, we arrived in this beautiful city, settled in a hotel and went to an address we had been given which was a shop in an old building. Several men and a foreman were established there, making gelatin molds over master ornamental models of cornices, which were to be incorporated in the new addition which was an arcade running through from one block to another.

I introduced myself and made myself acquainted with the work for which I had been commissioned. It was a group of four female figures, supposedly to be life size, but in the end became nine feet high.

My coming had been anticipated, and apparently had been looked upon as somewhat of an event for it had been reported in the daily newspaper. What concerned me most was the prompt arrival of the architect for the new building. He was a Mr. Keys, and he was decidedly intoxicated when we met. He wanted to see my model which I unwrapped and proceeded to explain to him. Then I had to describe something that he would have to imagine, to which he said "Hold on, I can't imagine anything. I want to be shown." He was not too intoxicated to question the dimensions which I had been given. My instructions had been very specific, for life-size figures, and my fee was based upon this, but he insisted they were to be nine feet high. With this change in the scope and amount of work it would be necessary to do, I refused to start work until I was assured that I would be properly recompensed.

Telegrams were dispatched to Chicago stating the altered condition, which brought a reply that a member of the firm, a Mr. Spindler, would come to Minneapolis to take up the matter with me. He arrived the following day. All our negotiations gained for me was a dinner for Mrs. Bock and me, and his promise for the additional amount to be paid to me upon completion of the work, because all I ever received was the amount of the original agreement.

The next person I met was the general manager of the store, a Mr. Powers, a well-educated and capable young man, son of the owner of the Powers Department Store in St. Paul. We found him a delightful friend and were his guests a number of times at his club. Mr. Powers planned a program for advertising the gala opening of the new arcade. As the Olson store was a large advertiser, the newspaper cooperated wholeheartedly, and every day reporters from the two leading newspapers would call upon me for news stories. This publicity resulted in numerous callers coming to see me work, some to talk and some anxious to take lessons from me. Two young ladies I agreed to teach if they could find a suitable place in which to work. One was a Mrs. Bachkus and the other a Mrs. Woodruff. They worked seriously, and it was a pleasant experience. Another caller who had been a pupil of mine at the Chicago Architectural Club was a Mr. Arnold, and a man who showed me a brick upon which he had carved a copy of Thorwaldson's Angel of Light. It was exquisitely done and I advised him to pursue his talent.

Over all, our sojourn in Minneapolis was interesting. We were entertained by many people, and made a number of friends. Mrs. Woodruff, whose husband was the organist of the Episcopal Church, invited us to dinner in their very artistic home. After dinner they took us to the church to hear his extemporaneous practice on the organ. Sitting in the quiet, dimly-lit church, we were surrounded and engulfed in the music which was like an emotional flood of heavenly harmony made by the angels in the universe. It was one of the most moving musical experiences of my life.

On the following Sunday we were the guests of Mr. and Mrs. Bachkus, my other pupil, and we met another guest who was an expert on mushrooms. Minneapolis is a paradise for a mushroom lover, and we learned a great deal about them, and later made a number of short exploration trips looking for them in the fields and woods. This knowledge that I gained about the delicious edible fungus led me later to an almost disastrous end. Another guest was the celebrated sculptor, Thomas Crawford, who was responsible for the "Armed Freedom" figure in flowing classic drapery which graces the dome of the Capitol in Washington. We had many delightful social engagements which kept us occupied.

The grand finale was approaching and my work was nearing completion. According to the arrangements they were going to have a dedication and an offical unveiling. A speaker's platform was erected, about fifteen feet square and about six feet above the ground, with steps and railing around the platform. The block in which Olson's store was located was closed off to traffic and was filled with people. A full Brass Band furnished selected renditions and spotlights placed in strategic positions played light over the crowd.

The main speaker of the evening was Mr. Olson, who was not only owner of the store, but was Superintendent of Schools. He lauded the "Great sculptor, Richard W. Bock," and then introduced me to the gazing, cheering throng. The fun of this whole parody was that Mr. Olson was so visably intoxicated. So, with a fanfare from the band, and with the spotlights blazing on the statuary atop the arcade's arched entrance, and with all eyes following the light, the veil fluttered away in the breeze.

The papers the next day carried a full account of the proceedings of the previous evening, elaborating upon it, and Mr. Olson was delighted with the success of the event. The turnout of the public for the occassion was a "veritable ovation to art." Festivites for the opening of the arcade kept up for a whole week. My friend Arnold came to see me to make a date for our last dinner before our return to Chicago. I was delighted with the graphic manner he described my reaction upon being introduced to the public by Mr. Olson. I showed "about as much enthusiasm as an accused person being led before a firing squad."

Mrs. Woodruff, also expressed sympathy for my obvious discomfort, and thanked me for the help I had given her in modeling, and for the opportunity of working with me. Some years later I saw a display in a number of stores of some small ornamental objects with her signature, proof of the seeds of art falling upon fertile ground.

My partner, Mrs. Bock, active always when she can be of service, proposed a plan she wished to carry out. She would give a farewell dinner of her own making to the two plaster casters, Mr. Rhan the foreman, and his helper Mr. O'Brian, for their kind cooperation and consideration while we were guests in their shop. It was a delicious chicken dinner with wine and all the trimmings, cooked on a small gas plate in the shop. As a memento we gave them a photograph of the group we had all worked on.

So ended our sculpture holiday in Minneapolis. This whole episode has always struck me as containing the elements of a comic opera.

Figures for Olson's Department Store, Minneapolis

Chapter XI
1900-1901

New opportunities were waiting on our return to Chicago. A committee appointed by the Illionis State legislature was instructed to ask for bids for the erection of suitable monuments to commemorate the soldiers who had lost their lives on the battlefield at Shiloh during the Civil War. One main monument, the Illinois State Monument, was the object of the competition which I entered.

These competitions are eagerly sought by the granite monument dealers who submit their own designs. In this particular competition twenty-seven designs were submitted, including mine and one by an architect. I was represented by my friend Paul Cornell, son of the owner of the American Bronze Foundry and the majestic Hyde Park Hotel in Chicago. After everyone had described the merits of his own design, the architect got up and to my surprise, spoke in laudable terms of my design, saying there was nothing in any of the other designs which were offered that were worthy of consideration. The final result was that I was given the first prize of three hundred dollars and the commission to erect the monument I had designed.

My design was simple and impressive. It was a huge square granite shaft slightly tapering to the top. Draped over the top was an American flag as though carelessly laid there, and an American eagle at rest with his talons gripping the shaft. On the front of the column was a bronze panel in bold relief depicting a battle-field scene. My drawing, which was of large dimensioin, and designed for dramatic effect, showed floating in the sky another eagle. A jokester among the granite men inquired if that flying eagle was part of the monument, and if so, was it of bronze or granite?

A few days later, when I met in conference with the committee, they had come to the conclusion that instead of the eagle and flag, they would prefer to have a statue on top of the shaft, and so it was ultimately executed; a very simple statue representing the Mother of Illinois, holding a sheathed sword on her lap. Her other hand held a book resting upon the block upon which she was seated, indicating the illustrous history of Illinois and her honored sons who had played such an important part in preserving the Union. There was, also, an inscription below the front sculptured panel which was part of Lincoln's Gettysburg address: "The world will little know, nor long remember what we say here, but it can never forget what they did here."

Because I had been doing so much travelling in carrying out my last few commissions, it was necessary for me to find a new studio in which to work. I was fortunate in finding a place wonderfully suited to my needs, a large studio that had once been the studio of Steele Mackaye of theatrical fame.

It was now November and I was thirty-five years old. I figured if my

Model for the Shiloh Monument figure with the sculptor

luck held out I could depend upon thirty-five more years of service to my art.

At about this time another milestone event in my life occured, a starlet was born to Mr. and Mrs. Bock. It was a little girl, the most beautiful child, accounted by everyone, and recorded in a bronze tablet I made of her. A lady patron came in at this time to see me with reference to some work and asked to see the baby, and was enraptured with it and made this observation: "It is a pity that head is not on the body of a boy." It was an interesting appraisal for the baby became a very precocious child.

This lady, whose name was Smith, wanted me to make a portrait statue of her young daughter who had recently died. This required no imagination on my part for she was so absorbed in the adoration of her child that she knew every "bone" in her body, and moreover in places were there were no bones. I knew she would never be satisfied with anything but an exact likeness, so I made arrangements to make a death-mask of her beautiful daughter lying in a vault in Chicago's Rosehill Cemetary.

At this time I was working on the Illinois monument. I had first made working drawings for the shaft of the monument, for which the committee had been clamoring from the time I had been appointed to do the work. The drawings and lettering for the inscription were completed very quickly.

Since I had to make a working model of the statue first, and I needed a live model, Mrs. Bock was willing to serve, and as we were encumbered with an infant, we decided that the fastest method would be to make a plaster cast of her whole body. As I was an expert plaster caster this was a safe and easy task, but it is not so easy for the model. Wet plaster is heavy and cold, but as it sets becomes very hot, not enough to burn, but be very uncomfortable for the model. I worked very fast and took every precaution as timing is very important in plaster casting. The whole operation took no more than two hours, and gave me a permanent model from which I could make my one-quarter size working study. When that was accomplished, I dressed my life-size cast with the drapery I desired and then repeated on the small model.

My working model for the seated figure of the Mother of Illinois was soon completed, and the committee came to inspect it. They approved it enthusiastically so I could now go ahead with making the full-size statue, which was a figure approximately eighteen feet high. I modeled this figure directly in plaster instead of clay, and then made a plaster cast. I decided to do it this way because of its size and simplicity. The resultant effect would be all in its favor because the rugged surface of the plaster would be entirely in keeping with the nature of the subject, much more so than the smooth surface of modeled clay.

In preparing the plaster for the technique of modeling with it, glue size is added to the plaster. A very small quantity retards the plaster setting for as long as an hour, and the process also makes the finished plaster much harder than usual.

I modeled the head and shoulders separately from the rest of the figure in order to handle and transport it more easily for casting in bronze.

As the bronze casting would take quite some time, I applied myself steadily until the work was completed and the committee could come for another inspection and final approval.

Illinois State Monument, Shiloh National Military Park, Tennessee

When everything was completed and ready for casting the foreman and Mr. Berchum, owner of the foundry, came to my studio to decide upon the proper dismemberment of the figure in order to facilitate transportation and casting. Workmen then came and cut up the statue into various segments as I had marked them on the plaster surface.

My next task was the modeling in clay of the large relief panel on the front of the monument. This panel measured seven feet horizontally and five feet vertically. The modeling of so large a panel, and lettering, is a very exacting task, and required a framework and other auxiliary equipment upon a movable supporting stand.

I now began modeling the battle scene between the Confederate and Federal Armies. The model I used for all of the figures, first nude then clothed in the respective uniforms, was an eighteen year old boy whose name was Liebchen. He went on to become a well-known film actor under the name Stuart Holmes. He starred in a number of films and later became a respected character actor.[9]

All of the various heads and faces of the figures in the panel were actual portraits of my friends and neighbors. This gave them a realism that would have been unattainable by using purely imaginary variations in the faces.

There were still a State Seal and two torches to model and cast. My work took over a year to complete and the bronze casting took nearly a year.

It is a rarity when I mention the name of a granite man in complimentary terms, but the man who did the work on the Illinois Monument is one of them. His name was Pageau, and he had a son who worked with him. they were both kind, gentle souls. I always had the highest regard for the integrity and work of these men. We never had a moment of friction.

It was interesting that through them I received a commission to design a cavalry monument for the battlefield. It was a pentagon suggesting a hitching-post, with bronze panels on each of its five sides, commemorating that many regiments.

My contract for the Illinois Monument called for my supervision of its erection on the site in the Shiloh National Military Park in Tennessee. This necessitated making two trips to Shiloh. These trips were interesting experiences for they took me through the river country of Mississippi and Tennessee for the first time.

Major Mason of the Monument committee, suggested I take the river trip so I could enjoy the beauty of the Mississippi River and experience the romance of the transportation Mark Twain had described so wonderfully. It proved to be a picturesque trip which took two or three days. The trip began in Paducah, Kentucky where I saw the blue grass for which the State is noted. There I boarded a Mississippi Side-paddler Packet Boat. There were innumerable towns along the way and we stopped at most of them.

In many of the towns as we tied up to the wharf, the stevedores who were waiting on deck, would start unloading the heavy railroad ties which were part of the miscellaneous cargo which the ship was carrying. Each one of these giants would lift and carry off one of the ties which must have weighed from two to three hundred pounds as if it were nothing, carrying them on their shoulders and singing as they worked. It seemed like a stage performance.

There was one very disturbing occurance which marred the entire trip for me. Three young passengers were just returning from a lynching about which they openly boasted. They even had a momento of the despicable act — a finger of the victim. Aside from that the trip was pleasant and the food and sleeping quarters were excellent.

Unfortunately for me, this steamer did not stop at Pittsburgh Landing where I wanted to disembark. So I had to get off at Savannah, which was five miles from there. This made it necessary to obtain transportation to Pittsburgh Landing. I was directed to a man who took care of such transportation not infrequently. He, with an assistant, rowed me in a small boat for those five miles, and charged me five dollars for their pains. They took as many shortcuts as possible, at times through heavy bayous, one in particular through a wild and desolate stretch which made me wonder if I could trust my rowers. It was this territory which Grant's reserve army had to traverse in order to bring pressure in the aid to General Lew Wallace in his attack on Shiloh.

It so happened as fate would have it, the State of Indiana had erected a State Monument which was being dedicated while I was there, and at which General Wallace was the chief speaker. He took advantage of this auspicious occasion to defend his conduct against the charges which had been made against him in that historic battle, for which the press had criticised him.

The following day I left to return to Chicago by train. The station was ten miles from Shiloh, so I had to hire a horse and buggy with a driver to take me there. The roads were very muddy and we passed many small hamlets and farms with pigs of all sizes lieing about in the road.

Arriving in Corinth with plenty of time to spare before the arrival of the train, I walked about to see the town, and to my great surprise it had a private museum, free for all to come view the exhibits which covered many areas of historic interest. The owner of the museum was a Southern gentleman from whom I learned much about the surrounding countryside, for this place was the scene of another important battle between the forces of the North and South.

The train finally arrived and took me as far as Indianapolis, where I had to transfer to the train for Chicago. This train did not leave until midnight, so I had about an hour to wait. The station was dimly lit and empty except for myself and another gentleman. It was General Lew Wallace, who spent his time silently walking up and down the spacious hall, and seemed like a lost soul. I knew he was troubled about the events of the day, but whatever his military fortunes, his fame rests secure in his other attainments and his creation of the famous novel "Ben Hur."

The train finally arrived and we boarded it, he for his home in Crawfordsville, Indiana, and I for Chicago.

Chapter XII
1902-1905

I had recently been in correspondence with the sculptor Karl Bitter, who had been my friend since our student days in Berlin. He had been named Art Director for the planned St. Louis World's Fair, the Louisiana Purchase Exposition. I was pleased with his success for I was responsible for him coming to the United States.

I received a letter from him that he wanted me to do a sculptural group of three figures for the Missouri State Building at the Exposition. Other sculptors represented on this project included Charles Mulligan, with a group similar to mine, at the other end of the building; James Earl Frazer with a statue of Jefferson; Johannes Geler with a corresponding figure of Napoleon Bonaparte, and Ed Kemyes with several bears. I take particular pleasure in presenting this roster as a family group for I had been associated with these men in the friendliest relations for many years. This was a delightful commission in every way because of the enjoyment of the work and the pleasure of being with such congenial co-workers.

I received my contract and instructions of the nature of the work required for the group, and the architectural details in which it was to be incorporated, so once again my whole interest and effort was concentrated on this new project.

The first requirement was the idea and to furnish a design in an accurate sketch model which in its final size would include a standing figure seven feet tall.

My design showed a central figure seated on an elevated pedestal representing "Abundance" holding a festoon of fruits and flowers. At either side, at her feet, were small models of a locomotive and a ship. Standing at her side was a farmer in the attitude of wiping his brow with his handkerchief, and resting his hat upon the pedestal of the central figure. At his back stood a cultivator and a stalk of corn. At the opposite side was a standing figure of a horticulturist in the act of grafting a young fruit tree, a knife in his hand, and a basket of his grafting buds at his feet. A crowing rooster and a small tree stood at the back of him.

I shipped the model to Karl Bitter's office in St. Louis. He approved it and returned the model to me with no criticism or modification and I immediately started work on the full scale figures.

The work progressed speedily and well and it was soon completed, molds made, and the finished casts sent on to St. Louis. All except the figure of the farmer which was completed in clay.

It was early March, and when I left my studio one evening I planned to cast the farmer the following day. I was hopeful and confident that within a week all of my modeling and casting of the group would be completed.

The next morning when I was a couple of blocks from the studio I noticed crowds of people hurrying in my direction. Then I saw the street was criss-crossed with hose, and I heard the chugging of the old-fashioned horse-drawn steam fire engines. I hastened my steps, my heart pounding. I was apprehensive but did not wish to accept the possibility that once again I was to be the victim of fire. I arrived at the scene, joining the throng of curious onlookers, no one guessing I was involved in the disaster, or what it meant to me.

It was a sad sight, but the left side of the floor upon which I had my studio was the only part of the building not leveled to the ground, so later I was able to salvage a few precious tools and drawings, but my model of the farmer was a complete loss. Everything was caked with ice, which was the only factor which made it possible to save even those few things.[10]

After gazing at this destruction for about a half hour oblivious of the cold, I returned to my mother-in-laws home where we were then staying. When I came in the house my wife was still in bed, but hearing me she sat up in alarm fearing some catastrophe, for she knew I had intended to start casting. With a smile I said "Well it's done. It is all finished." I then related, as calmly as possible, the scene which I had just left. My mother-in-law, hearing my story inquired if I was in my right mind or suffering from shock, for I was not emotionally lamenting my loss.

Actually, I could not afford to waste time in lamentation and had already formulated in my mind the next steps I would have to take. First of all, I needed more time to model another figure to replace the one which had been lost. I communicated my calamity to the commissioner in St. Louis, asking for an extension of time, which was granted. My next step was to see my friend Charles Mulligan who had a large studio, to ask if he would permit me to model my figure in his studio. He very graciously granted me this favor.

A new farmer soon resulted, like his prototype. This figure was completed within a week, and was if anything, better than the first. It was cast and sent off to St. Louis.

I soon had to follow to St. Louis to oversee the installation of the whole group in place. My being on location resulted in a request from my fellow sculptors working on the same project, to look after the installation of their work as well. My former pupil James Frazer was there, also, and gave me a hand with the work. We had a very enjoyable reunion for after he moved to New York we had not seen each other for a number of years.

Beside his figure of Jefferson on the building, he was also represented by another splendid figure of an Indian holding a long spear, astride a horse. Both the rider and the horse were in a very dejected pose. The title of the work was "The End of the Trail." It was a masterpiece, the most commanding figure on the Exposition grounds, and it became famous, with thousands of reproductions in all sizes. Frazer is probably best known for this figure, though he created many splendid works including the design for the United States five cent coin, the Buffalo Head nickel.

When the Exposition opened in the spring of 1904, my sister Marie invited Mrs. Bock and me to be her guests for a week's visit at the

Detail, Missouri State Building Louisiana Purchase Exposition, St Louis

Exposition. We took our small daughter in a perambulator, and she was very impressed by the pretty Japanese dancers.

The most spectacular display was a high, illuminated tower with a cascade of water. The tower was about one hundred and fifty feet high and at the sides of the watersteps were numerous sculptural figures, a very beautiful highlight, most of them done by Hermon MacNeil. In the "Court of the States" Lee Laurie was the most prominently represented among the sculptors. This Exposition, in general plan and Baroque design, not withstanding its lavish use of sculpture, could not compare with the classic Greek design of the Omaha Exposition.

After our holiday week of sight-seeing we returned to Chicago. On our arrival I found a notice of the death of my dear friend Roberto Raskovich, and I was very saddened. I felt he had never recovered from the separation from his wife and child. I recalled I had been with him one time at twilight when he played some very sentimental nocturnes on his violin, and some of Schumann's music, and I noticed tears falling from his eyes. I remembered how he had told me frequently "My dear boy, you don't know . . ." But I did know.

After completing the "Boulder" for Wright in 1898, I became too busy to see much of him, and he was doing some work for which he did not particularly need me, but we saw each other often, whenever there was an opportunity. We would have dinner together and our families were close. After dinner he particularly enjoyed playing the pianola in the children's playroom. On this instrument he would render Wagnerian music, as the "Fire Dance" and some of the Valkyrie music, in magnificant style.

Wright had some very interesting commissions to do during this interlude, including the Dana House in Springfield, Illinois, the Larkin office building in Buffalo, New York, and residences for some of that company's officers.

As I had been busy and not available during this time, Frank was obliged to find someone else, and the sculptor who was working with him was a man named Vandenberg, a talented but eccentric artist without any basic training. He wore his hair long and had a long beard cut in the image of Christ. He did not have a studio and Frank had established him in the octagonal drafting room at the studio. This made the studio very crowded and somewhat confusing with the conversations being carried on all around, so a change had to be made.

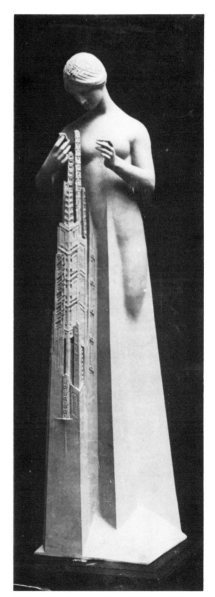

Frank called me in to straighten out the dilemma. He wanted me to do a standing figure for the entrance of the Dana house that Vandenberg had started but was unable to continue. Frank's idea for the figure was well conceived but far from solved. When I took it over there followed a long and tedious effort, in which as usual, we frictionized and fraternized, often coming to the verge of tears in our arguments for Frank could not make up his mind how it should be done. He was still under the thrall of Sullivan's style which I worked very hard to break down. So we were building up and tearing down constantly. Finally he was called out of town on business for a number of days. During this time I was able to finish the entire figure. When he returned and saw what I had done, he beamed and threw his arms around me "You have done it" he exclaimed, "You have done it, Dicky, you have done it. This is going to make you famous." I was overwhelmed with so much praise, and really tired to exhaustion with the strain of completing the figure before his return, and I told him he could have it, I was through with it.

This figure, the Dana Figure, really became the keystone to the Wright Style, as he himself has admitted; and as to my fame in connection with it, I can only say that some years later when he had an exhibit at the Chicago Art Institute, that figure and other of my work was included. It received only disapproval from those who were critical of Wright's tenets, for I was struck with the same stick that was used on him. So much for my fame.

"Flower in the crannied wall" Frank Lloyd Wright Dana House, Springfields, Illinois

There was another piece of sculpture for the Dana House which awaited completion. It had been started by Marion Mahony from a sketch I had made. She was a fine draftsman and all around artist. She was a brilliant intellectual and a match for Wright in debate and argument. She served as a source for practice and criticism for his lecturing in which he became a master. He was sarcastic and he used biting and caustic irony. In debate he endeavored to rattle his opponent, and then shoot his adversary's argument full of holes. We often took on each other which we both thoroughly enjoyed.

In the album of Wright's work, Mahony's hand often offered a great contribution, which was acknowledged and appreciated by him.

The sculpture she had started for the Dana House from my sketch was a rising full moon filled with happy children's figures. Miss Mahoney's splendid interpretation of this small sketch was to be used as a wall fountain in the Dana House, and needed a lot more work for completion. I called this fountain "The Moon Children" and when completed, like the Dana Figure, it was cast in terra cotta.

Model of "The Moon Children" wall fountain in the Dana House

The following Christmas, this elaborate and artistic home of Mrs. Susan Lawrence Dana was ceremoniously opened to her friends and guests. Mr. Wright's staff and his whole family and my family were also invited.

I had been busy studying and making sketches for the Larkin Administration Building to be built in Buffalo, New York. It seemed impossible for me to escape Frank's influence in spite of my occasional revolt against it, for I admired his work, and he was a dear and good friend.

The Larkin building was under construction, and when Frank was going to Buffalo to oversee it, and make a short trip to New York, I decided to accompany him. We arrived at Buffalo, and after seeing the building we called at the office where he asked for and received about fifteen hundred dollars advance on the work. We then went on to New York and stopped at the Belmont hotel, the most modern hotel in the city at that time. Frank decided we were going to have a good time which started with an opulent dinner. The next day he contacted his cousin Richard Jones who invited us to have dinner with him at his club. We spent the afternoon shopping, mostly browsing through a Japanese print shop. Frank was a collector of prints and when times were hard he would sell some at a good profit. At this time he was looking for a particular print to complete a series, and he paid over seven hundred dollars for it. To an untrained eye it appeared to be the simplest picture imaginable. I bought what I considered a more attractive print for which I paid the sum of seventy cents, which amused him very much. Apparently I had not made such a bad choice, for when we got home he discovered my print also belonged to one of his series, and he offered me another in exchange.[11]

When we finished our print shopping and kept our dinner engagement with Dick Jones, there was not much left to detain us in New York. I had called a few friends, including James Frazer, who again urged me to move to New York. We stayed overnight and returned to Buffalo the next morning. After settling the hotel bill, and arriving at the station, Frank found he was too short of money to buy the tickets, so it was up to me to pay for them, which was not an unusual situation between us.

Arriving in Buffalo we went immediately to the Larkin Building where his advice was urgently needed on the construction. Paul F. P. Mueller was the building superintendent, an able engineer, one of the finest men in his field. My interest, of course, centered upon the sculptural features for which the stone was being placed in positon; the carving was to be done after the blocks were in place. A new building material, magnesite, was being used on the interior, for both floors and walls. It is a sound and fire proof material, and Frank was especially interested in that.

One evening we were invited to have dinner with Darwin D. Martin, secretary of the Larkin Company, for whom Frank had designed a home, another of his architectural gems. The outstanding feature of this home was a mosaic fireplace, used as a wall. The motif was a wisteria vine in full bloom, done in varicolored glass mosaic. The beauty of this panel is indescribable.

I had done two pieces of sculpture for the garden of this home. They were horizontal blocks, five feet long by two feet by two feet. These blocks were articulated by life-size children. One represented Spring with playing children surrounded by dogwood foliage. The other represented winter with the children asleep under a blanket of snow.

The trip had been enjoyable and I was stimulated by the work that was to be done. Back in Chicago I first made sketches of the two pier terminals in the shape of globes about seven feet in diameter. In front of each were two kneeling boy figures. On each side of the piers were descending bands. The nature of these designs is impossible to describe adequately. The other pieces were two large panels about eight feet square which were to be placed at the two entrances to the building. Each entrance had a pool with water flowing into the pool in a sheet from beneath the sculptured panel. There were also articulated ornamental blocks with characteristic Wright designs in spaces between the windows at the top story of the building.

Inside the building there were two five foot square panels on each side of the fireplace. Each showed a winged figure resting its arms upon vertical tablets. I designed these panels which bore inscriptions and were of an unrealistic character like those for the pools.[12]

The models were completed and sent to Buffalo for the stone carvers to use as patterns. The building would take about a year to complete.

Exterior Panel, Larkin Administration Building, Buffalo, New York

Interior Panel, Larkin Administration Building

I had engaged two stone carvers, one of them, Mr. Baumgarten was a very fine carver. He was to do the two panels and the other carver did the work at the top of the building which was plain and did not have as much fine detail. Mr. Baumgarten had built a shack with a stove for heat, in which to do the carving during the bitter Buffalo winter. When I visited the building the following spring I was surprised at how little I had to do in finishing pointing up. Frank was also well pleased and had no criticism of the work.

Unfortunately, the terrace groups of Spring and Winter for the Martin home had been delayed so the office building could be completed. Now that it was finished I could give my full attention to this work. These also were to be carved in stone. I had had time for the study of these delightful groups, and it did not take me overlong to complete them. Mr. Martin had felt at times that he would never get them and was pleased to see them for they were a most important and necessary feature in the architectural design of the residence.[13]

The Larking Building marked a turning point in my thinking. I had to decide my future. It was a question of whether to be or not to be continuously associated with Frank Wright.

I had been pursuaded by many of my friends in New York that it would be to my advantage to locate in New York City. So I decided that, with the Wright contracts assuring a good beginning, I would do the Larkin work in Buffalo where it was to be placed, and it would still be under Frank's observation as he oversaw the construction of the building. If it seemed right, the next step would be to move to New York.

While I knew my action would not please Frank, I saw no reason why I should sacrifice my independence to his pleasure. I went to Buffalo to investigate the possibility and look for a studio, and then I wrote to him about setting up my studio there, explaining my reason in a logical manner. However, he became very angry, and wrote that he needed me near him for constant consultation, and threatened to terminate my work with him if I did not return to Chicago.

This developed into a stalemate for both of us. I held out for three months, and when he came to Buffalo he put more pressure on me, and appealed to our friendship, finally resulting in termination of the argument in his favor.

However, I did set up a studio in Buffalo for three months and moved my family into the new Statler Hotel. This sojourn left many happy memories for Mrs. Bock and me. We visited the Roycroft Studio in East Aurora and called upon the founder, the famous author Elbert Hubbard. Our daughter who was then four years old, immediately made friends with him. She sat on his lap and told him stories of her own invention. She was very outgoing and made friends with everyone.

We visited Niagra Falls many times, viewing all of its stupendous beauty. Also, we saw other places of interest in the vicinity of the city, usually picnicing in the open, and wishing it would never end. William Drummand, the Chicago architect, and his wife were in Buffalo for a time, and they often accompanied us.

But we did not go to New York; we returned to Chicago.

Mrs. Richard W. Bock

Chapter XIII
1906-1908

We were two happy families, Wright's and mine, and we saw each other very often. We were now living in Maywood, a suburb about two miles west of Wright's studio in Oak Park. On Sunday, I was in the habit of walking from my home to Frank's. Seemingly we never saw enough of each other. One Sunday morning, passing through a large vacant field in River Forest adjacent to Oak Park, I saw a large Giant Puff-Ball mushroom which is delicious, and another mushroom which was umberella-shaped, and I thought an edible variety.

I presented my find to Mrs. Wright, and she was delighted, never doubting my authority on mushrooms. She suggested I stay for luncheon and she would prepare my find for us. So we had our repast and relished my donation.

When I left home it had been with the understanding that I was going to call on my mother who lived in Chicago. I had intended to stay at the Wright's for only a minute or so before continuing my journey. After we had our lunch I continued on my way which required a long streetcar ride. On the way I had a very peculiar sensation, a strong taste of mushroom in my mouth that because very noxious.

I had barely arrived at my destination when I became very ill. I was put to bed and the doctor called. The retching and vomiting was accompanied by a paralysis-like stiffening of the limbs which was intensely painful. The doctor gave me medication, and during a calm moment I directed him to call Mrs. Wright to tell her of my distress. The doctor learned from Mrs. Wright what I had feared, that her Frank was in the same condition, in great agony and under the care of a doctor. Fortunately, Mrs. Wright had not partaken of our feast. It was decided I should stay overnight with my mother.

With my reputation as an authority on mushrooms shattered, I was an ideal target for some of Frank's barbs. The thing that had done the dirty work was the umberella-shaped mushroom, one of the many poisonous varieties. It was years before I ate mushrooms again, and I never saw Frank eat one.

One time I received a call from Frank. He and Mrs. Wright were down town, and he had been given tickets to the theater, so he invited Mattie and me to have dinner with him and Mrs. Wright and then attend the play. We accepted, and left our little daughter with the Wright children, something we often did. We had dinner at a fine restaurant in the Pullman Building, and when we had finished and the waiter brought the check, Frank, very nonchalantly handed it to me. I mention this not as a reflection upon him, for he could be the soul of generosity, but as part of his eccentric character, which I accepted.[14]

He liked to tease, and would say, smiling "Dicky, you know what's the matter with you? Too much Mattie and lemon cream pie," my favorite dessert, then he would laugh uproariously.

One time I met Frank at his down town office on a very hot summer day. We went out for lunch together and he felt as I did when he suggested we go to a restaurant where they had excellent beer. We ordered beer and emptied the mug at one draft, which seemed like only a teaser. I wanted another and so did he even though he never drank beer. Then, he made one of his typical jokes "Dicky, you shouldn't drink beer, but I guess you always will, being German." I challenged that remark, telling him I would prove I did not have to drink beer. From that day on I have rarely had beer. I had already given up smoking at my wife's request.

One Sunday afternoon, my wife and daughter and I had tea with the Wrights and afterward they accompanied us back along Chicago Avenue in River Forest to Thatcher's Woods, a beautiful wooded area along the Desplaines River. Chicago Avenue at this time was still a country lane without sidewalks. When we came to the Soo Line Railroad tracks, I was walking on the inside where there was a depression, and Frank, always being up to some deviltry, gave me a shove and when I stumbled into the depression he remarked in high glee "That's where you belong," and he was right, for that was the identical piece of property I bought and where I built my studio and home.

People were beginning to acquire automobiles, so Frank was one of the early possessors of this contraption — a bright red Studebaker touring-car. One evening when I was staying late at the studio, he offered to drive me home in his new mechanical buggy, saying it had been guaranteed to run sixty miles an hour. The road was perfectly straight, one mile from his studio to mine. Cranking it up, there were no self-starters then, we started on a wild ride as he proved the car's speed. We arrived safely though I was in a much shaken condition. A short time later he broke his arm cranking the car, so the joy rides were over and he did not drive again for a long time.

Wright had been preparing himself for the art of public speaking so he could present his thesis about architecture to the world. His premise was that "Form follows Function."

He wrote, he talked, he preached and he debated the subject, especially to his office force. When all of his thoughts had been clarified and written down, it was in the form of a long scroll. Isabel Roberts, who worked in the office, then typed it up in a more presentable form. This manuscript "The Art and Craft of the Machine" was presented to the public for the first time at Hull House in Chicago, one of the first Settlement Houses in the United States.

At this meeting were Miss Jane Addams, founder of Hull House, Professor Lubin of the University of Chicago, Hugh M. Garden, Birch Burdett Long, the office staff, Mrs. Wright, Mrs. Bock and myself. Small though this attendance was, it was a challenge to the world for his theories had been launched and were now widely publicly debated. The lecture was written up in the press and his theories have in due time spread over the face of the globe.

For the sake of the record I will list Wright's studio staff at that period as I remember them. They were Walter Burley Griffin, Marion Mahony, William Drummond, Barry Byrne, Charles E. White, Isabel Roberts, Schindler and Willie.

Unity Temple, the Unitarian Church in Oak Park, Illinois, was then under construction. Paul F.P. Mueller was the contractor for this magnificant and unique structure, the first of its kind made entirely of reinforced concrete. It was a veritable monolith, for which I made the model for the ornamental columns. Mr. Charles Woodard was the chairman of the building committee. Without him it would not have been built for he had the ability to visualize the structure and then see it become a reality. From the beginning he had a tug of war with the congregation which did not approve for it was too revolutionary and unlike any other church in the world.

At the time the Unity Temple was being built I was also commissioned to design a drinking fountain "for man and beast" in Oak Park. This fountain was to be erected at curbside at the Oak Park and River Forest Park, with funds raised by a horse show. Mr. Woodard was also the head of this committee. My design was a center shaft with sculptured panels on each face, a flower box on top, and a trough-like base for horses and dogs to drink. I showed my design to Frank and asked how he liked it. He looked at it at length with approval, then he made a suggestion, took a pencil and poked a square hole through the center shaft, changing it to a double shaft. "Now Dicky," he said "You've got something." That is the way I completed it, sculptured panels on the inner faces.

Oak Park Fountain

The only difficulty was that now he began to lay claim to the whole project, and so stated to the committtee. Mr. Woodard came to my rescue, stating publicly that the Oak Park, River Forest drinking fountain was mine alone. This fountain is still claimed for Wright by some writers about his work. As for me, I feel flattered he would wish to claim it, and would ask for no better tribute.

I will always remember the happy family life this many-sided, contradictory character had at this time. He loved and understood children, and he and I thoroughly enjoyed our growing families. One winter day Frank received a large barrel of fresh oysters from a client. A party was quickly arranged. Tressel tables were put up in the studio, and it was fun to watch the jubilant children roasting the oysters in the fireplace and serving them to the guests. There were seven children, with Lloyd the oldest, directing the others; and even our five year old daughter carried a basket and helped gather up the empty shells.

The Wright children loved to play with her for she was so unlike them. She was dainty and fairy-like, a born actress. She would sing and dance impromptu, gesticulating and telling stories of her own imagination, completely unmindful of any audience. Frank especially enjoyed her and called her Dolly. Frank's two daughters, Catherine and Frances, would dress her up in various costumes and Dorathi would love it for it gave her an opportunity to do another act. Catherine was eight years older and Frances, who was three years older, loved to tease her, and sometimes she had to be rescued.[15]

Llewellyn, youngest of the Wright children, and my daugther's birthdays fell on the same date although he was three years younger than she. Every year they would share their birthday party with all of the accompanying festivities which are dear to the hearts of children.

Those were happy and trouble-free days for all of us.[16]

January, 1907 was an important date for us for this was the day Thorwald Methven Bock came to us. Preparations for Thor's birth had been made with the family physician, Dr. Emily Luff. That afternoon a very severe blizzard started and it would not be many hours before the roads would be impassable. We kept in constant touch with the doctor by telephone, and decided she should not delay her arrival any longer. Even so she had great difficulty driving her faithful horse Betsy the two miles to where we were then living in Maywood. Driving through the raging storm, plowing through deep snow drifts and the almost impenetrable wall of the blizzard, she finally arrived. The nurse that had been engaged did not arrive until hours after the doctor. Years later, Thor, an appropriate name for the god of war, who arrived in such a storm, grew up to be a very peaceful and handsome boy, and a talented artist.

Dr. Luff was a kindly person and a lover of humanity and animals, and she befriended all. She was also the Wright's physician. When he went to Japan regarding the commission for the Tokyo hotel, he took his mother with him, and he engaged Dr. Luff to accompany her as her companion and to look after her health.

We enjoyed listening to her account of that trip, which must have been interesting. But she received little enjoyment from it, for she did not like anything about the country or the journey. She said she was getting too old for such adventures, and no doubt she missed Betsy and her other pets. On Wright's first trip to Japan Mrs. Wright had accompanied him, and according to her later reports she, too, had derived little pleasure from the journey.

Portrait of Thor

Chapter XIV
1909-1915

Almost two years had passed since Thor came to us. He was able to walk and beginning to talk. He was the sweetest baby, and very handsome.

We had purchased the heavily wooded property in River Forest, and built my studio at the rear of the land, with the plan of building the studio Frank had designed for me in another area.

In 1910 the album of Wright's works to that time was published by the German publishing house of Wasmuth in Berlin. This book was distributed widely over Europe and greatly hastened his world fame.

Among the plates was the drawing of the studio Frank had designed for me, and which was one of the finest in the album. But this studio was never built, and as of this date, if there be a heaven and if I get there, I pledge myself to ask St. Peter for a building permit to construct it, which would make heaven really worth while.

I had a number of commissions to execute and shortly after they were completed, Mrs. Bock suggested that we move from the house we were renting into the studio and live there for a short time. After her suggestion we started immediately to work on the living quarters. A boulder fireplace from rocks found on the property, cement foundation, sidewalks and a reflecting pool, sculptured panels from the Larkin building, etc. These were all incorporated in the building from the foundation up, causing me to state "Here we build a house that is surrounded by sculpture as an integral, essential part of the architecture instead of an afterthought decoration which is often eliminated for the sake of saving money, leaving an uniteresting shell as a building." In the course of later additions more sculpture was added. An important feature of the building was the horizontal leaded glass windows, a gift from Frank. They had been removed from his studio during some remodelling and we placed them high like clerestory windows with wide sills under them upon which we placed small sculptures and blooming plants.

It was a great disappointment to me that the Wright studio was never realized, but it is no boast to say that our little studio home at Chicago and Forest Avenues in River Forest, became a local landmark, and frequently was taken as a Wright house by young architectural students making a pilgrimage to the locality of the famous Frank Lloyd Wright.[17]

About this time two important events occured in Frank's studio. First was the completion of his country estate, Taliesin at Spring Green, Wisconsin, where he later installed Mrs. Mamah Bothwick Cheney as mistress, which changed the course of his life forever; and the second involved two members of his studio staff. A romance had developed between Walter Burley Griffin and Marion Mahony through their collaboration on an international competition to design the capital city

Drawing of Frank Lloyd Wright's Studio for Richard W. Bock

of Canberra in Australia, and its government buildings. This competition carried a first prize of $25,000, and it was a supreme surprise in architectural circles when they won first prize. An acknowledgement of their success was given by the Chicago architects in a banquet where they were toasted and many speeches made in their behalf. Everyone wished them success in their great opportunity. Good wishes were indeed needed, for their task, because of interference and obstruction by local political and native architectural factions, became very difficult.

"The Gnomes," the home studio in River Forest

They had nothing but trouble with the work, and their marriage became a nightmare. Walter Griffin gave up and became a real estate salesman, and Marion Mahony returned to Chicago.[18]

Also at this time two gentlemen from Japan came to Wright's studio to confer with him about building a hotel in Tokyo. They later engaged him for the project and the hotel was built and became one of the wonders of the world, withstanding several severe earthquakes.[19]

I was engaged to create a seasonal display of decorative sculpture for windows of Marshall Field's Department Store. Charles Frazer, a Frenchman and a fine art director, was head of the display art department. We collaborated very harmoniously, and it was an enjoyable outlet for me with my early training in the decorative arts. During my association with Fields, which lasted for five years, these displays drew national interest and acclaim for works in this field. Fields had several dining rooms, and I also designed a central fountain and a bronze lamp of a standing female figure with a small Tiffany globe, copies of which were put on every table in the Prompeiian Tea Room.

My work frequently required live models, and a strange incident occured one time when I had a beautiful female model. She posed for quite a time so I had an opportunity to learn something of her background. She had an irritating cough which she said was the result of thoughtless students while she was posing at the Chicago Art Institute. They insisted upon keeping an open window which resulted in her catching cold which developed into tuberculosis. Her name was Hubbard, and she was the niece of the celebrated Elbert Hubbard, for whom she had little regard as he had ignored a plea she had made for help.

After I had completed this series of sittings, weeks passed and then one day a lady called to see me. She said that she had taken the liberty of calling to see me on behalf of Miss Hubbard who had spoken so well of me. A series of unfortunate crises had resulted in Miss Hubbard commiting suicide. Being absolutely penniless, her burial was a serious problem in which this friend was seeking help. I assured her I would do all I could.

I related the problem to Mr. Frazer and everyone in the department generously donated. I went to the Art Institute and received a contribution. With my contribution I was able to raise sufficient funds to give this beautiful and innocent victim an honorable Christian burial. Mr. Frazer had one of his men take charge of the arrangements. The funeral was on a dull drizzly day, as if the heavens were weeping over this unfortunate soul. There were few mourners, and Mrs. Bock brought a large bouquet of wild flowers from our garden which she laid upon the grave.

Sometime around 1912 the Midway Gardens Company was organized to build a place of amusement, fittingly called San Soucie, to be designed by Frank Lloyd Wright, and to be built at 61st and Cottage Grove Avenue in Chicago.

I was to do the sculpture work, and as there was a great deal of sculpture planned, I was obliged to look for some assistants. This took me to the Art Institute and my friend Charles Mulligan, then head of

Field's display Wall Fountain

the sculpture department. I told him of my quest, and when I had finished he took me by the arm to show me the work of a young artist recently come from Poland, named Stanislaus Szukalski. His work was unique. Mulligan considered his work "Crazy," but I was amazed at the highly individual work and considered him a genius.

I was introduced to this artist, and told him I needed help at the Midway Gardens, and if he was interested I would have him meet Mr. Wright. As I was then serving on the committee for the National Painters and Sculptors Exhibition, I advised him that all of the pieces he had, consisting mostly of heads, very bizarre in treatment, should be entered, together with his many drawings which were outstanding.

The jury was composed mostly of out-of-town artists, and when they examined his work for inclusion in the exhibition they marveled at his exceptional craftsmanship. However, since it was an exhibition of sculpture and paintings, the drawings could not be accepted. They recommended that he enter the drawings separately in the Water Color Show which came later in the year, or that he should have a private exhibition of his work in a One Man Show. They gave him a letter to the Director of the Institute recommending such a show.

With this highly complimentary letter, he went to the Director who allocated a choice small gallery in which to hang his works. I happened to be in the Institute at the time the exhibit was being hung, and being well acquainted with the guards, I was permitted a private preview of this unusual exhibit. I then went on to view other works. A few minutes later when I was passing Stanley's exhibit again, the guard approached me, and in a mysterious low tone, and pointing to a picture standing on the floor, told me that Mr. Goodman, one of the Institute's Associate Directors, had just been there and removed the picture from the wall. Stanley had followed him and observed this unusual act, and was at that moment in heated discussion with the Director about this outrageous breach of authority, for all of the works had been passed by the Board of Directors. He reminded Mr. Goodman that no one but the Board, or the Chief of Police had the authority to remove a picture if it were deemed offensive to the public. However, in order to relieve the Director of any further embarrassment he would immediately remove the entire show, which he did. The picture which the Director had removed showed the British flag as a spider web.

I was so impressed by Stanley's unquestioned genius that he became my protege, and I did all I could to assist this amazing talent to be recognized. He spent a great deal of time at my studio and with my family, and we all became very close friends. He did have a fine career, and contributed many splended works of sculpture to the world, including his native Poland.[20]

As plans for the Midway Gardens progressed I had Stanley meet Mr. Wright with the idea of having him work with me. He called upon that genius, and from what I learned later from both sides, I regretted I had not been present at the meeting. Apparently it was just short of being an outright case of fisticuffs as their personalities struck sparks immediately, and only proved that two geniuses on one job would be one too many. However, Frank was able to find a very suitable and talented young man, Alfonso Iannelli, an Italian from California, with whom I was well pleased.

The site for the Midway Gardens was soon humming with activity. The first thing to be erected were shops in which to work. All of the structural ornamentation was to be cast in cement, as well as the sculptural features. Many monolithic pieces were required, and of course, they first had to be modeled in clay. Waste molds were then made from the resultant casts, and gelatin molds made for duplication.

The building was constructed of Indian red brick and grey cement. The main piece of my work was a huge monolithic block approximately seven feet square. This block had a group of five figures in bold relief on its surface. The center figure which suggested wings and a checkered gown might represent Mephistopheles, and under his wings two youthful figures on either side, each holding a suspended string of confetti of different angular shapes. At the corners were the suggested forms of long-bearded old men, all carried out in angular, fantastic forms. The whole mass was interspersed with angular, confetti-patterned blocks. The design of the entire block resembled the character of this main panel, and was in fact, my particular character of design, which had its inception with the original Dana figure and had evolved into this personal, individual style. I must state with regret, that this ingenious conception was never properly displayed as it was used as a pier on an inside stairway landing, its true beauty lost in the inadequate artificial lighting.

Model of the Monolith for the Midway Gardens

There were a number of other pieces I had to do, such as a vertical panel, five feet by eighteen inches, with an alternating checkerboard design. Before the design had been approved I had already made two other designs from Wright's sketches, but time was pressing as there was a deadline to be met. The resourcefulness of Paul Mueller in expediting work brought about the making of wooden molds of the characteristics of the general design and proved to be very adequate, saving a considerable amount of time.

The task of creating an idea into tangible form, the unique creation of a great architect, was a formidable undertaking. Fortunately, Wright had been able to work with one of the world's ablest craftsmen, Paul F. P. Mueller, contractor for the entire project, without whom he would have had an immeasurably more difficult time. Mueller understood Wright and his ideas and knew how to carry them out for they had worked together for years, from some of the greatest works of that first great master, Louis Sullivan. Wright and Mueller appreciated each other for their skills.

Wright's great love for horizontal lines which float so easily on the drawing board, and represent a dramatic extended roof-line, presents a most difficult task when reproduced in concrete. It was Paul's job to solve these engineering problems which developed, and to anchor the great masses of concrete and steel so they would securely float in space as Frank visualized them.

Time limits were an important factor in the construction of the Midway Gardens. It was Paul Mueller's task to fashion and build a full city block of brick and concrete buildings in a span of ninety days. It developed after construction was well under way that the project had not been adequately financed. Mueller then stepped into the breach with $200,000 which he was able to raise from a Mr. Seips, his partner on this contract. This enabled the Gardens to be completed, though it took a number of years before the last of the subcontractors were completely paid off.

From the very first we were harrassed by the walking delegates of various unions, who kept a watchful eye on our operations, seeing to it that it was an all-union enterprise.

Neither Iannelli, who made the model for a pier figure which was duplicated across the front of the building, nor I belonged to a union. We were designated as Independent sub-contractors and did not have to be union members. However, a tipsy plain-plaster union delegate insisted that we join the union or else all work would immediately stop. Frank wanted to treat the incident as a joke, but only succeeded in fanning the flame of the defiant agent who had little regard for art. I came to the rescue, having once before been forced to become a member of this same union when I was twenty-one years old and doing some decorative work. For the time being, I told the agent, Iannelli and I would join the union, and to prove our good intentions I made a down payment of five dollars for each of us toward membership.

This settled the whole flurry, the agent was happy for he had gained his point, and the work was able to continue. A week later I went to the

Modelers' Union Hall where they returned my ten dollars and apologized for the trouble caused by the agent.

If I were asked what I thought of the whole concept of the Midway Gardens, I would say it was an artist's gigantic dream, fresh, vital, forceful and full of imagery. It is this quality which we artists often sacrifice in the serious afterthought of practicality, when a concept becomes laborious and just another task. The whole Gardens suggested a dream of happiness, and every one of the innumerable people engaged in the enterprise, the artists, laborers, carpenters, all deserve credit for the part they played in making it a reality. I salute Frank Wright and Paul Mueller for this extraordinary achievement, an artist's dream come true.

The Gardens had a grand opening on schedule, with a band for dancing and the National Orchestra under Max Bendix. But there was still much to be done: decorating, furnishing and planting. Only the interior night club was open the first year. The complete Midway Gardens opened on July 3, 1915 with the great Russian ballerina, Anna Pavlowa and her company, as the premiere attraction.

The Midway Gardens was a wonderful success until it was given a mortal blow by the passage of the Volstead Act in 1919. All the hopes and expectations for this beautiful garden restaurant – music hall, were dried up with the enforcement of prohibition, and it was impossible to continue. It is now only a memory. What a pity that we destroy so much of what we should preserve.

Frank toyed with the idea of an amusement enterprise on the lake shore which was of stupendous scale. I made numerous drawings for it, but at the last moment it failed to be realized.

Other forces were now at work in Frank's life. As for his transgressions, and his falling in love with other women, he has himself made a clean breast of it, and humbled himself before the world. I do not deem it fitting to pry into the private affairs of other people, even though this one touched me so closely, and so shall not mention it further. He has paid a heavy enough price.

I would like, however, to say a few words on behalf of Mrs. Catherine Wright, who was bereft, but maintained a steadfast dignity in the face of public scandal. She was pestered day and night by a hoard of reporters who came knocking at her door and even climbed through a bedroom window to steal family photographs to feed a curious public. She asked one such party to come in and talk. "Yes," she said, "I am the wife of Frank Lloyd Wright, and I am the mother, as he is the father, of our six children, all living. Do I, or do I not, owe such innocent ones consideration? What would you advise? Should I add fuel to the morbidity of the press and public and harm them more?" He was a chastened reporter when the interview concluded, and he apologized for his intrusion.

She was a warm and lovely lady, and Mrs. Bock and I tried to sustain her during these trying times. Our home, too, was overrun for a time by those seeking gossip.

Dr. G. V. Black
Father of Modern Dentistry

When Frank went to Tokyo to build the hotel he expected me to go with him, but times had changed and I did not feel I should leave my family for the extended length of time it would require.[21]

The architect Charles E. White, Jr. was building a home in Oak Park for the Skinner family, and he asked me to drop in and see him about some sculpture as he had allotted space for some art work in his design.

The first was a panel over the fireplace. I did the work in bold relief representing two classic seated figures with a tripod alter in the center from which incense vapor was rising. The other work was an interesting garden pool and fountain. I spent considerable time and thought on this project, more than the architect had expected of me, his idea being along the conventional "cupid on a rock" type, which I immediately discarded. In this endeavor I was fortunate to be working with the fine landscape architect Jens Jensen, whom I had known for a number of years. We discussed my ideas and he came to my studio to inspect what I had done. During the formalities of our greetings, he kept eyeing the fountain group in the background. Then, viewing it more carefully he turned to me and enthusiastically agreed that it was the perfect solution and most appropriate for the design he envisioned for the garden.

Beside the center feature of articulated architectural design I accented the four corners of the pool's rim with similar designs. In the background at either side of the pool, I had Hermes standing in among the flowers. The whole was in perfect harmony with nature and the owners were enormously pleased.[22]

"Skinner Fountain"

Chapter XV
1916-1919

We were members of the Prairie Club, a group of nature lovers who enjoyed hiking on the dunes, and joined with others in an effort to save this unique area by making it a State Park. The Dunes are located at the southern tip of Lake Michigan where the boundries of Michigan, Indiana and Illinois share the lake shore, each having a portion of this dune country.

Wind, water and time each contributed their portion to the formation of this area of huge sand hillocks, some three and four hundred feet high, and great blowouts, like huge bowls which may change from year to year. These moving dunes shift so that an area that had been a blowout one year may be a high dune the next. What makes this area unique is its vegetation. In a part of the country known for extremely cold winters with freezing blasts from Lake Michigan, tropical plants and even desert animals thrive there.

Great cottonwood trees, with gnarled trunks and twisted branches brave the onslaught of the forces thrown against them, surviving even after having been buried up to their crowns in sand. Other vegetation also dares to survive upon scant soil. Clumps of bunch grass, even cactus and a delicous ground cherry as well as patches of wild blue berries abound. There are shifting streams, fashioned by nature's unpredictable force, where the lover of fishing may cast his line among pads of beautiful water lilies and water hyacinths from a shore lined with cat tails, reeds and marsh mallow. In sheltering nooks varieties of fern and wild orchids

Portrait of Thor

grow, nestling around the trunks of sassafras and huge tulip trees. Wild life of numerous kinds survive, some of which are indigenous, but there are land and water birds, mammals, lizards and snakes even including the desert rattle snake. It is heaven for nature lovers and they come from all over the world to study the phenomena.

There is also a rare quaking bog covering a large underground lake. In this area vegetation is found in tropical profusion, including trees with trunks three feet or more in diameter. If one stands on the roots at the base of one of these trees and rhythmically jumps up and down it will cause wave motions on the surface of the bog, so that over a wide expanse the ground undulates and the huge trees sway upon their unfirm foundation.

We often went to the Dunes on Sunday, getting off the Illinois Central train at Porter and walking over the Dunes to the lake. Then we would hike along the shore. In season my son and I would take a tent and trappings, and spend a week or more exploring and enjoying its unique pleasures. We would select the wildest part of this secluded area. We supplemented our meals at "Fish Johnson's" a commercial fisherman who lived on the lake shore and carried a stock of groceries as well as serving delicious fish dinners in his small fisherman's hut.

When we first went there the Dunes were almost a virgin wilderness with little human encroachment. In a five mile stretch of beach there were no more than a dozen cottages and the Prairie Club, a small building on a high point. At intervals along the shore were scattered fishermens' shacks with all their paraphernalia of nets drying upon racks, and boats where they had dragged them upon the shore.

One year Thor and I dug out of the yellow sand an old relic part of the keel of a ship, which was about ten feet long and ten inches square. When we prepared to leave we wrapped our tent poles and bedding around it and shipped it back home, where it was planted upright near the entrance gate. On the top I fastened a weathered horse's skull we had picked up on one of our trips of exploration. It served for many years as our totem pole.

The Dunes were always an ideal place for artists of Chicago and vicinity, and they were always well represented in paintings and drawings at art exhibitions.

In 1916 a movement was started to stage a huge pageant to raise money to help make the dunes a State Park.

Plans were well under way when a murder was committed, and a phantom was seen walking on the Dunes. The result was, of course, that the Dunes were prominent in the press for weeks. Reporters and law enforcement officers were at the Dunes every day and they finally caught the phantom, a young woman who had tired of city life and went back to nature. She was immediately put under arrest for murder, but was found innocent and warned to live a more conventional life in the future; but the Dunes had been well publicised which helped the pageant.

The pageant was staged in the spring of 1917. Over a hundred people took part including a number who were well known, among them Thomas Wood Stevens who wrote the drama on the history of the Dunes, and

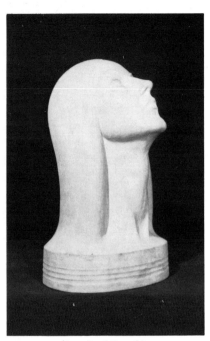

Portrait of Dorathi

Donald Robertson, the Shakespearean actor, who directed. Mary Wood Hinman, the noted folk dance authority was in charge of the dancing. She was the teacher at Columbia University who shocked the country when she took the bulky bloomers off girls in the dance department and put them in more aesthetic costumes. My daughter was the solo dancer in the pageant and even my son participated as one of the little Indian boys.

The pageant was a financial as well as artistic success, and the Dunes became a State Park, saved for posterity. However, over the years civilization has drastically changed the Dunes, and I lament the virginal wilderness that I first knew.

My work has always been my greatest pleasure, and I was fortunate to be busy during the years of the First World War when art was largely neglected.[23]

Some of the works I recall doing during this period included a call I received from the well-known architect William Gray Purcell who came to my studio in the summer of 1914 to secure a piece of sculpture for his home in Minneapolis. I offered to loan him a piece, a baby child of the goat-footed creature the Greeks called a "faun," but better known as "Pan." This was one of a pair I had done for Marshall Fields. But the proposed place for the piece was an unusual one with a diagonal axis, and called for special treatment. After some study we mutually decided to do a figure of Nils Halgerson, the Goose Boy, from the book by Selma Lagerloff I had been reading to my children. The piece was very effective, as the boy astride a goose with outspread wings in full flight seemed to be flying into the room from its high placement, and took its place in one of the early houses of contemporary organic architecture. The Goose Boy became one of my most popular sculptures and was widely displayed.

When Mr. Purcell moved to Philadelphia in 1917 he took Nils with him for his new home. Unfortunately, the piece was destroyed in a train wreck. We had decided to make a new casting when just at that time World War I came to an end and Mr. Purcell moved to Portland, Oregon. A new casting was made and a place especially made for it in the new house he built there.[24]

I also made a terra cotta fountain for the house Mr. Purcell built for his father in River Forest.

The Devoe Paint company was erecting an office building in Chicago for their extensive business, for which Arthur Waltersdorf was the architect. We had been friends since childhood, and he spoke to me in regard to doing some architectural sculpture for the facade of the building. He had confidence in my ability and left me to design all of the decorative features.

The building was seven or eight stories high, divided into four vertical pillars of glazed terra cotta, rising from the first story which was of polished granite. The piers terminated in three youthful sculptured figures holding hands. These supported the upper structure of the building. The different floors were divided by ornamental panels and several of the floors included flower boxes on the window sills. At approximately the second floor, on either side of the front of the building was a bracket-like Indian head nine feet high by three feet wide, done in an unusual art nouveau design.

All of this work was done in the shops of the Northwestern Terra Cotta Company, but as I did not belong to the union of the working staff, I was not allowed to do my work in the shop's studio and had to rent a store directly across the street. They made an exception for the large heads, and were gracious enough to overlook the regulations permitting me to use the shop studio. The Devoe Building was a distinctive sculptural and architectural unit, modest and unpretentious for all its artistic merit, the only one of its kind in the city.

I remember a small job I did for the Riverside Golf Club in Riverside, Illinois, for the architect William Drummond. It was a panel in bold relief of a figure of Pan, seated in a crotch of a tree. He was holding a golf ball in his hand as an invitation to play, and he wore a mischevious smile. My son Thor, who was nine years old at the time, posed for this figure. The panel was five feet high and twenty inches wide and extended about sixteen inches from the wall which was of brick.

I modeled this interesting panel directly on the wall, upon a board which was temporarily fastened to it. In this way I could best judge the appropriateness of the design in its proper setting. It was easily removed for casting, which was done in cement. When this had been accomplished, the panel was securely fastened in place. I further enhanced this cement relief with gold glass and colored irridescent glass mosaic.

Nils, the Goose Boy (2nd version)

This quotation

> "Who does not love life, wine and song,
> Remains a fool his whole life long."

as you know, was by Martin Luther, and is what I interpreted for the architect P. J. Weber, for a new front he was creating for the Kau Wine Stube Restaurant on Wells Street in Chicago. There were two white clay terra cotta panels, one showed a standing monk holding a glass of wine in one hand, and a pitcher in the other, with the suggestion of a wine barrel in the background. The second showed a singing female figure with a harp. There were also other panels, one with a quail and another a lobster. These small panels were incorporated in the wall of the building. At the top of the entrance at the side were two characteristic heads. The interior had some very interesting wood carvings.

Sometime later I had another interesting commission from Mr. Weber. It was for a door for a columbarium for a Mr. Fisher. I designed the door which was cast in bronze, of a female figure in very high relief, heavily draped and holding an urn which is also draped. In the center of each side of the building at the top were dolphin's heads carved in stone and polished. I also designed a bronze casket to hold the ashes of the deceased Mr. Fisher. It was six by ten inches in size and heavily decorated over its entire surface.

One day a mural painter named Lichtgarn came to see me about doing some decorative sculpture for the chapel at a Catholic church in Chicago. He had been commissioned for the entire project and I had been highly recommended to him. The work he wanted me to do consisted of two pilasters in Italian Renaissance style, ten feet high and fourteen inches wide; also a frieze of cherubs around the ceiling. To impress me and show his good will he paid me five hundred dollars on account. When the work was completed he paid the balance on my contract, and as he had also completed his work we shook hands and parted.

A few days later I received a letter from Father Johnson, the pastor of Loyola Church, asking me to see him. The first thing he asked when I entered was whether or not I had received payment for my work, and I assured him I had, which seemed to puzzle him. He then revealed that when Mr. Lichtgarn started his work, he had been very concerned about the safety of a package of pure gold leaf which was to be used in his ceiling painting, and which he said was very valuable. He requested the pastor to keep it in the safe, which was done. He then told me they had just discovered that the material which was used was not gold leaf, but was what is called "Dutch Gold" a metal substitute of little value and for which he had paid the painter the price of pure gold.

I was of little comfort to the Father as Lichtgarn had given me fair treatment, except he had torn a picture from a rare book I had loaned him, and he had taken one of my cabinet-maker's planes.

Following the First World War and for a number of recovering years the country experienced a period of great prosperity and I had a number of interesting commissions.

I received a call from my friend Arthur Waltersdorf about a memorial entrance to an athletic field which Mr. Louis Hippach was presenting to the boy's school at Farmington, Maine, in memory of his son, a star athlete at the school who had lost his life in an automobile accident.

When Arthur showed me the design it was brick post and wall at either side of the entrance, with an inserted panel with an inscription. I took him to task, asking him what was distinctive about it that made it a memorial? He agreed, and I suggested he should have a sculptural panel on the brick wall at each side of the gate. He was pleased with the idea and gave his approval. These panels which were modeled in bold relief, were seven feet long and five feet high, showing youthful standing figures, representing football on one side and baseball on the other. They were cast in cement and were an appropriate memorial to a young man.

Fisher Columbarium

Chapter XVI
1919-1929

Following the War I had a number of commissions commemorating that unhappy event. One was a very conventional statue made as a civic monument for Jersey City, New Jersey. It was a realistic charging soldier with a fixed bayonet, titled "Over the Top," symbolizing the spirit of the First World War. In a small size about four feet tall, it was widely copied for schools all over the country.

I also did a five foot tall standing figure of General George Rogers Clark in bronze for the Daughters of the American Revolution Memorial Building in Washington, D.C.

For the Elks Convention in Chicago I had a commission from the Chicago Elks through the architect Alschlaeger. This was to do two huge elks, almost twice life size, which were to be placed on top of two pilons, over fifty feet tall, located at Monroe and Michigan Avenue next to the Art Institute.

The process in making these huge figures was difficult because of the heroic size of the finished figures, and I had very little time in which to complete them.

First I made a working model, one-third life size, cast in plaster. On this model I drew lines dividing it into different sections, the divisions being made upon horizontal and vertical lines, with the neck and head in one piece and the antlers being separate.

Templates were then made to follow the contours indicated on the various divisions. The templates were then enlarged to the size required for the finished figures. Large wooden armature frameworks were then made, conforming to the general contours of the smaller segments. The edges of these sections incorporated the enlarged templates so that a perfect match and conformation would result when the completed parts were assembled in their proper positions.

I then modeled directly upon these frames with plaster of Paris, mixed with a binding material such as jute and hemp. This modeling followed the working model. The head and separated antlers were modeled in clay and then piece-molds were made. For the base and legs I constructed a framework of inch-thick steel rods. The whole project was completed, assembled and erected in place within the allotted time. Putting them in place was a difficult and hazardous operation, requiring extension ladders and a derrick to lift the heavy figures onto fifty-foot high concrete bases. I had helpers and we worked all night getting them in place. The next morning was Sunday and I was anxious to see how they looked in daylight. I wished to get a view of them from a distance as that is the way they would be seen, so I went to the steps of the Art Institute. There I met the registrar, Mr. Tuttle, who shook my hand and complimented me for they really were a thrilling sight, those two huge elk standing so proudly.

General George Rogers Clark, D.A.R. Memorial Building, Washington, D.C.

There should have been a civic movement to have these beautiful elks cast in bronze and placed permanently, but no such movement was initiated, and after the convention they stood for a time and then were removed, although the bases still stand. I was obliged to pay for the placing and removal of these figures, which alone came to well over six hundred dollars, so that with my other expenses I received not one cent for my work.[25]

I was introduced to a Judge Walter Meyer, who seemed to wish to be friendly. He was of German descent and belonged to the German political group in Chicago which was formed to reestablish their prestige which had been damaged by the anti-German sentiment during World War I. Their activities centered around a building project, with the historic name of Baron von Steuben of American Revolutionary War fame. The building to be known as the Steuben Building was completed with funds subscribed, but there were complications and many unpaid debts because subscribers did not fulfill their pledges.

Elks Monument

The judge had kept in touch with me and one time invited me on a junket a group was making to the northern part of Wisconsin. The purpose of this gathering was a political rally to discuss the choice of a candidate for mayor of Chicago. There was a considerable amount of drinking and card playing on the train, in which I did not participate. This went on during the night and the group detrained the next mroning in high spirits. Of the twenty or so present, I knew only Judge Meyer, and I later met Otto Becker and Dr. H.N. Bundeson who was their choice for candidate. I was asked to model a relief portrait of him which was to be cast in bronze and presented to him. I was pleasantly surprised when Mrs. Bundeson recalled she had posed for a head I had modeled of her when she was a teen-aged girl.

The place where we stayed was a summer resort without a name, and it was to be named Steubenville. To commemorate this decision I was asked to make a portrait of the property owner. I was later paid for both of these portraits.

This kind of gathering was a new experience for me, and one of its main pleasures was meeting Otto Becker for we became good friends. Sometime later I learned he was one of two members of the art committee which was in charge of a new administration building to be erected in Chicago's west side Garfield Park. The other member of the committee was Susan Small, a sister of the then Governor of Illinois, Len Small. These two had the authority to recommend the artist to do the sculpture for the interior of the building. I was chosen by Mr. Becker and Miss Small, and the next step was to receive the approval of the Commission and sign the contract.

I will never forget the ordeal before this approval was accomplished. I had to wait in the Commissioners' office day after day in the terrific heat of a Chicago July. However, it was probably all for the best for they got to know me before we met for we sat looking at each other through the open doors of the committee room. The importance of this small incident exemplified a dictum I learned from Judge Meyer, "Keep yourself always in the picture."

My patience was finally rewarded, and when at last I saw the Chairman, Dr. Robertson, and the Board, it was almost routine to obtain their approval and sign the contract.

One of the purposes of the sculpture on the interior of the administration building was to glorify the regime of Governor Small, who was known for the development of good roads in the State. This was to be depicted on four large sculptural panels. I also modeled a portrait relief of the Governor to be incorporated in one of the panels and for which he posed. Fate played one of its peculiar capers, and before that particular panel was finished Governor Small had died, and the portrait was omitted.

I called upon Dr. Robertson and saw him alone in a large committee room. He spoke to me at some length upon the vageries of political fortune. When I inquired about the portrait of Governor Small and its placement in the panel, he replied "The King is dead, long live the King." However, fate was not through, for within two months, Dr. Robertson himself, was gone, ending his ambition to become governor.

Model of one of four panels in the Chicago West Parks Administration Building, with portrait of Governor Len Small

Michaelson and Roggenstadt were the architects of this beautiful Baroque building with its golden dome. It seems improbable, but before the building was completed, Mr. Roggenstadt too, had died.

My work, however, continued and consisted of four large panels in a circular rotunda, to be executed to fit the curvature of the walls which were of Travertine, Bavarian Rose and Italian marble. The curved marble walls, polished in this articulate form was an accomplishment of most excellent craftsmanship. My task was even more difficult.

The first of these five by seven foot panels, cast in cement to represent Travertine, depicted architecture and sculpture, the second panel represented the hardship caused by bad roads as affecting the farmer; the third panel represented transportation, and the fourth, recreation. The bronze inserts on these panels were in each case, a circle superimposed upon a square.

The panels had to have a slightly concave curvature to conform to the curvature of the walls of the rotunda in which they were to be placed. I modeled them in clay as flat panels and then made waste molds from which casts were made and from them gelatin molds, which were then placed upon a template support which conformed to the wall curvature. the gelatin molds being pliable took on that curvature, as would the casts made from them.

The casting of these four panels in cement to represent marble was an interesting technique. Travertine in the original is a richly veined Italian marble of a yellowish tone, and in order to simulate it different colored batches of cement were mixed which would conform to the original colors, then pieces of floss were dipped in them and scattered in the mold. The large mass of yellowish colored cement was then poured in, filling all of the remaining space. When set, and removed from the mold, this cement had all of the appearance of real Travertine marble. However, they required considerable pointing up and finishing before being installed in place in the wall. They were washed with a 50% solution of muriatic acid, polished with abrasives and constantly seasoned with water by being kept covered with wet cloths. The inserts of bronze and stone had, also, to be incorporated in the panels in their porper positions, and when this was done, the work was completed.

I received two more commissions from Waltersdorf. One was for a monument for his family cemetary plot at Forest Home Cemetary near Chicago. It consisted of a huge slab of flesh-colored granite, covering four lots, with four headstones slightly raised from the surrounding surface. Rising from the center of this plinth was another slab standing on end, and carved with lettering on one side. On the other in an incised low relief was a portrait of Arthur and his mother, she seated and he standing protectingly over her. To one side was a faint, abstract portrait of his father. On the narrow sides of this slab was incised a weeping willow tree.

The last commission I received from Arthur Waltersdorf, perhaps the most important and significant of all, took two years to complete and was climaxed by a lawsuit.

I was called into consultation by Waltersdorf in reference to a project upon which he was working for Louis Hippach, for whom I had

Bronze Urn, Hippach Memorial Chapel

collaborated with Walter for the boys' school gates in Maine. This was for a chapel in memory of his parents. Walter and I had been long time friends and he entrusted me with creative freedom, so I feel the monumental character of this building is due in part to my influence, and I acknowledge with gratitude his placing such trust in me.

The chapel, in Chapel Hill Gardens West, in Villa Park, Illinois, presents a plain high-pitched roof, the walls are of fitted various-sized blocks of sandstone, while the windows are Gothic design in leaded amber-colored glass. The main feature of the structure is a square tower with a porte cochere connecting it with the building at the main entrance.

Here I placed a memorial urn, standing upon a slab of granite. This bronze urn is five and a half feet tall, and holds a record of the important world events of the 1920s. The main feature of the designs which cover the entire surface are eight panels showing man from the cradle to the grave. Above the continuing arches which separate these panels are a row of portrait heads of the world's great philosophers and religious prophets. The character of the urn is an egg-shaped pattern as I planned to make it universal in style. There are earmarks of half a dozen different styles, but the general feeling of the whole design is Gothic. At the foot of the urn are three basins from which water flows in cascades from one to another representing the River of Life.

Hippach Chapel Urn in situ

Hippach Memorial Chapel

It took me over a year to complete this one object. Casting the urn was a difficult task, and it was done by the lost wax process.

Half way up the surface of the tower, which is of Colorado white marble, are three five by six foot panels, one on each of three walls. The one on the front depicts a young female figure leading a young man to the mysteries of the Beyond. The side panels are the same size and of a conventional decorative design. A little higher on the tower is another panel representing an angel, showing a head around which is a suggestion of wings, the whole being in a diamond shape. There is no indication of feathers on the wings as it is purely decorative in treatment. These heads are repeated on all four sides.

The top of the tower is an open belfry, in the style of an articulated Gothic arch, containing a carillon. The tower terminates at the top with a parapet between the four corners at which there are over life-sized figures leaning over the edge with their arms resting on the cornice. These are also treated in an angular style, and represent a bearded male philosopher, a hooded woman, a shepherd and a young maiden.

In the interior of the chapel exposed beams terminate in corbels, four on each side. These corbels are heads carved in black walnut, each one different and representing different ages. These heads have arms which are holding shields. Being of such a dark color, and in the dimly lighted interior they were completely indistinguishable. Neither Walter nor the painter would take the responsibility of heightening the color of these details, so I took it upon myself and painted them, then rubbed them down bringing out the highlights. The effect was entirely in keeping with the rest of the interior. The ceiling is a mural and so is the end wall over the alter. On either side of the alter are bronze tablets depicting kneeling angels holding wreaths.

At the rear of the building are the graves of Mr. Hippach's parents. At the foot of these graves stands a Hermes, shaped like an obelisk, and so designed that there is a suggestion of wings and other symbolic designs representing life.

All of my work was completed and I came to what should have been a pleasant termination. I called upon Walter to determine the value of my work, there never having been a price set from the beginning for my work continued to increase as the building progressed. I had never made a point of a contract as I thought our long friendship precluded any serious differences, and Mr. Hippach had expressed himself as thoroughly delighted with the completed work.

It was late one afternoon when I called upon Waltersdorf in his office, and he immediately broke the tension by saying "If you think you are going to get ten thousand dollars out of this, you are damn badly mistaken, and you can sue for it."

I had not mentioned a price, and I made no reply for I considered his remark an ultimatum to which no reply was required. We then spoke of casual things and he suggested we go to dinner at the Blackhawk Restaurant, which we often patronized, and business was not mentioned again.

The following day I called upon the law firm of Gross and Rooney and explained the situation. They immediately brought suit against Waltersdorf and Hippach, which took a number of months before it came to trial.

Of course this did not delay the dedication of the Chapel on September 15, 1928, which was attended by a large crowd. During the ceremony Arthur took full credit for everything. Paul Mueller, who was standing with me during the ceremony, was amazed at the oversight, for I who had contriubted so much, received no recognition.

About this time I received a communication from Mr. Ellis Lawrence, Dean of the School of Architecture and Fine Arts at the University of Oregon in Eugene, Oregon. He was inquiring if I would accept a professorship of sculpture at the University. If it was agreeable he would call upon me in my studio in River Forest.

I met him by arrangement, and we talked over his proposal of my taking the Chair of Sculpture the coming fall. My trial with Waltersdorf was an obstacle, and I acquainted him with it, so that when the trial came up I could absent myself from classes and return to Chicago. This was agreed upon, so I accepted the position.

There was an attractive commission which went with the position:

to create the sculpture for the Campbell Memorial Court which was to be part of the Museum of Oriental Art being built on campus. Campbell was a former president of the University.

On our way to Eugene Mrs. Bock and I stopped in Los Angeles for a short visit with our children, and arrived in Eugene in ample time for the opening of the 1929 Fall Term. We found a very pleasant apartment, and I was confirmed as Head of the Sculpture Department at the first general faculty meeting. At that time I had just passed my sixty-fourth birthday and regretted that I was not younger, for the obligatory retirement age was sixty-five.

The city of Eugene, Oregon, in 1929 was an exquisitely charming place, a typical university town surrounded by hills with the Willamette River on one side, and a mill race flowing through the center. The landmarks on either side of the city were two very high buttes: Skinner's Butte and Spencer's Butte.

The sculpture department studio area was especially roomy and pleasant, and I was determined that I would give the students a thorough groundwork in the techniques of sculpture, which I had learned through experience and my studies in Europe.

A short time after I arrived I was given a bit of advice by a well-meaning instructor, who told me how important it was to keep in favor with the faculty. A faculty member should remember that his positon was social and recreational as well as to teach, for if he were too conscientious in his efforts to instruct the students it might reflect unfavorably on others.

Classes started and I was pleased with the size of the enrollment. I started work on the drawings for the Campbell Memorial Court, and Mrs. Bock and I did a lot of walking to become acquainted with the city.

My teaching method was very thorough and professional, but academically unorthodox. My classes were very popular and attendance greatly increased. A practice of mine which went against the norm, was that I gave grades as much for effort as for excellence. A slow student who tries his utmost in effort needs encouragement and appreciation, and sometimes in the end they turn out to be the most gifted. Of course this upset almost everyone.

The most distinctive thing about this charming small city was the Mill Race, a beautiful smooth-flowing body of water about ten feet deep, which wound through the center of the city, past overhanging tree-covered banks which gave the city an Old World character. Houses lined the shore and the streets crossed it over small arched bridges.

At the "Anchorage," a rustic, romantic restaurant popular with the students, the Mill Race was about thirty feet wide. In the spring at this point bleachers were put up along the bank when the students held an annual Water Carnival. All of the various fraternity and sorority houses and other campus organizations competed in designing and building large decorative floats which then passed the reviewing stand, propelled and guided by swimmers.

The Carnival theme varies from year to year. Our first year in Eugene, it was based upon fairy tales. It was a rule that no more than ten dollars might be spent upon each float, and it was wonderful to see how ingenious some of the students were. Many of my students designed floats for their groups, and one of them, Dorothy York, designed the float for her sorority house which won first prize. It was a huge polar bear with the head and neck designed so they could be moved by means of cords. Riding upon the back of this bear was a beautiful maiden.

The pageant was held in the evening, and the shore was festooned with lights, and the floats were illuminated. Colored flood lights were placed upon the bottom of the stream. It had a most wonderful fairy-like quality. The pageant had other features beside the floats such as music, swimming and diving exhibitions, and finally a long line of all the canoes, one person in each, holding on to the canoe in front so this long train glided soundlessly and effortlessly through the intricate windings of the stream propelled only by the accompanying swimmers. It was delightful and memorable.

Another student custom which took place in the fall at the opening of the football season, was a noise parade. Every conceivable article and method of making noise was utilized: backfiring autos, blowing of horns, beating on iron boilers by husky students with hammers, etc. The climax of this parade was a rally and the burning of a huge "O" high on the side of Skinner's Butte. Due to the traditional rivalry between the University and the State College at Corvallis, it was carefully guarded until the moment of lighting to prevent its being set off by their rivals. If all went well, the noise parade ended at the foot of the Butte, then, with music and speeches to cheer them on for the coming game, the evening was climaxed by the huge flaming "O" seeming suspended in the sky above them.

Chapter XVII
1930-1932

In the early spring of 1930, my attorney's advised me to come at once as my trial with Waltersdorf/Hippach was to be called in a few days. Accordingly, I made arrangements at the University for a two week leave of absence.

My wife and I arrived in Chicago in ample time for the opening of the trial which was conducted by a circuit court judge whose name I have forgotten.

In conference with both sides it was decided instead of a trial by jury, to leave the decision of the case to the judge.

I had but one witness while the other side had two. One of their witnesses was an official of a decorator's supply company, and the other was an ornamental modeler. My witness was the sculptor Emory P. Seidell.

I was very fortunate in my selection of attorneys, for they quickly discredited the other side's witnesses. But my witness was not much help so the case depended upon Waltersdorf and me.

The night before the trial I had written down a number of questions my attorney should ask the opposition witnesses, which he followed in his cross examination. One of the two witnesses in particular, a Mr. Gentech, the modeler, when he was examined the point was stressed as to his expertise as a judge of my work. After a few questions he admitted his outstanding achievement had been a wall fountain for the new Palmer House Hotel, consisting of a lion's head spouting water, and with that he was dismissed.

My witness, Mr. Seidell, an able sculptor, became so nervous he was not able to answer questions.

Then it was Mr. Waltersdorf's turn to be questioned, and in his cross examination my attorney, Mr. Rooney, used an unusual tactic. After the perfunctory questions about himself and his being the architect of the chapel in question, he was asked to tell of the various styles of architecture. This the witness did reluctantly, and bruskly asked what that had to do with the case, offering the opinion that I wanted to give the impression I was the creator of the chapel. With that he was excused. When he sat down, Mrs. Bock, who sat not far from him, overheard him remark "Where did Bock get those attorneys?"

It was now my turn to take the stand.

After the usual preliminaries, I stated that at the present time I was professor of sculpture at the University of Oregon, and that I was the creator of all the sculpture on the chapel; that Mr. Waltersdorf and I had always been the best of friends and that I regretted the present situation.

I was asked in cross examination what I thought of Mr. Hippach in my dealings with him. I replied that he was a likable man, friendly and pleasant, that this noble act of building such a beautiful chapel as a memorial to his parents was admirable.

I was asked if it was not true that Mr. Waltersdorf had provided me with considerable work which I answered in the affirmative. They asked me to name another architect for whom I had worked, and I named a score of them, including the work I had done for Michaelson and Roggenstadt of the Garfield Park Administration Building. Then the question was asked as to what my political pull had been to get such a job? That question brought me to my feet as I turned and faced the judge, while at the same time an objection was raised by my attorney. The judge had the question stricken from the record. With that I was excused. Again Waltersdorf was heard to remark that his lawyer should never have asked that question.

Immediately after that the attorneys summed up their cases. Again, I remember that our side presented the best case. After the summatiion the court was dismissed for the day while the judge took the case under advisement. The next day court was convened for the lawyers only. The judge decided in my favor, but not for the whole sum which I had claimed. It was, however, larger than I would have been willing to accept from Waltersdorf if he had been fair about the whole matter. I accepted the finding of the court, but the other side appealed, which delayed the settlement for many months.

I was now free to return to Oregon, and we immediately left.

When the Appelate Court completed its examination of the case and handed down its decision, they not only approved the finding of the lower court, but went out of their way to compliment me upon my work and the fairnesss of my claim. Mr. Waltersdorf and Mr. Hippach did not carry the case farther but settled, including all court costs and the interest which had accrued.

Upon my return to Oregon, I immediately resumed my classes and work for the Museum of Oriental Art. My classes were all that really mattered, and the results were more than gratifying for I soon had an enrollment of over eighty students. Before I came to the university the maximum enrollment in the sculpture department had been three students. The Dean had hoped I would build the department, and I certainly had made a spectacular start.

One day I was asked by the Dean to give a talk on sculpture to the student body in the auditorium. For this I selected a number of slides from the files and had some others made. One of these was of the celebrated group by the French sculptor Frimiet, showing a gorilla carrying a woman, called "The Abduction."

I had written a short sketch on this group for a magazine in Oak Park, Illinois, and for the climax of my talk I read it to the students. They could relate to this macabre seduction and enjoyed it immensely.

Monday was the day the Dean came to the University to have lunch with the faculty at the Ancorage. The luncheons were pleasant and I made friends and enjoyed them. Everything was going very well and the Dean was happy with the way his beloved Museum was progressing, and with the enthusiasm and attendance of my studentss some of whom were really outstanding.

My own private studio was open all day for the students to drop in and talk and see how I worked. Beside my work on the Museum and classes, I also modeled figures in the life classes, and my criticism and assistance was available to the students at all hours.

In the class in portraiture, which the students had formed of their own volition, the model was always one of their own group. This extra curricular class met at night, and I always met with them for I felt that such enthusiasm deserved all the encouragement I could give.

One of the models for this group was our studio janitor, Billy Rivers, who had a very interesting, gnarled face. I made a striking likeness of him and gave him a plaster cast of it, for he had performed many extra chores for me out of friendship, and I kept a copy for my collection.

My department had been running very smoothly, and I had trained one of the students as an assistant who could relieve me of some of the more laborious work, such as showing beginners how to cover a board with clay upon which to model.

The class had progressed to the point of learning the technique of making plaster casts from their clay models. There is no modeling class that I know of, either here or in Europe, which teaches plaster casting along with the modeling techniques. In schools, when the clay models are completed the clay is thrown back in the box to be used again, practicing modeling only as an exercise. Yet, plaster casting is an interesting and very important part of sculpture and it is a technique that must be known if the object is to be cast in bronze or some other material. Otherwise one must pay someone to do the job.

For economy I conceived the idea of a mass demonstration. I made up a class of about twelve students who would all do the same thing at the same time that I was demonstrating.

I procured the necessary articles for each student: suitable tin pans, a knife and tablespoon, a couple of bottles of vaseline, some dry powdered ochre color, a bottle of water glass which I diluted half and half with water, a good-sized pan to hold dry plaster and one for water, and small boards of the same approximate size upon which the students would model a clay design of their choosing.

For the demonstration I invited Dean Lawrence to watch the class, and the staff photographer to record it. There was, also, a large group of students who came to audit.

This is the way I taught the class how to cast their clay models in a permanent plaster material.

"Class ready? First we are going to make a waste mold.

"Grease the board around the edge of your clay model with vaseline.

"Now take a pan and grease the inside of it. Fill it half full of water, add a teaspoon of the dry yellow ochre powder and stir. Take the spoon out and dry it, then use it to scoop up the dry white plaster. Notice how I do it, by sprinkling the plaster lightly over the surface of the water so lumps do not form. Keep adding plaster until the pan is filled to the top of the water. Now stir so the mass is evenly mixed and the color is even. We now have a mixture resembling heavy cream. We will wait a minute to give the plaster a chance to react. You will notice that it has started to thicken slightly.

"Take a spoonful of plaster and apply it to the model, keep on applying until the model is covered to a depth of a quarter to a half inch evenly all over. Work quickly as it starts to set. The plaster will now take from ten to fifteen minutes to harden, or set, giving us time to clean up our equipment and work tables.

"Let me mention in the process of waste mold casting, if we were making a large piece, say a life-size head, and we had our layer of colored plaster, as we now have, we would have to add the addition of an extra strengthening layer of white plaster over this.

"Now we return to our casting. The plaster is hard so we raise the plaster from the board. Turn it over and remove the clay. You will be able to remove the clay with the spoon handle or with other tools if the work has fine detail. When the clay has been completely removed we will apply water glass with a brush to the inside of the mold. This is a separator. We must allow this to rest for a few minutes. It is applied to prevent absorbtion of water from the plaster which will soon be applied to make the positive cast. I want to draw attention to several other separating mediums and methods. The mold may be soaked in water to the limit of its ability to absorb more, or the mold may be coated with soap; yet another process is to paint the inside of the mold with several coats of thin shellac. This last, however, requires a wait of from ten to twelve hours to let it completely harden, otherwise it has a sticky surface, and requires a special grease with which to grease the mold.

"Our mold is now ready and we can resume our work.

"Once more we take our tin pan, grease it, put water in it and mix our plaster as before, but without the color.

"I want to mention that in plaster casting timing is of the utmost importance; you must concede that the plaster is the master. Every action from the beginning, after placing the plaster in the water, and for fifteen minutes after, all that you want to do and how, must be clear in your mind before you start. You must comply with the nature of plaster as it sets quickly and there is no way to go back and rectify a mistake. A slip of any particular part means diaster for your whole effort.

"We return again to our small model. The plaster in the pan is presumably just right to pour into the mold. Do so, and then, after vigorously shaking to remove any air bubbles which may have formed upon the surface of the mold, pour the plaster back into the pan. Doing this just once is sufficient, for now the plaster will start to set quite rapidly and we must work fast to replace the plaster once again in the mold before it hardens too much to be tractable.

"We now have a few minutes while we wait for the plaster to harden. So I will tell you how we change the setting nature of plaster so we can speed it up or delay it as circumstances dictate.

"If we want to speed up this setting process, as I do when I make a life mask, we add a little salt to the mixture, which should be added to the water before the plaster is added. However, if we wish to retard the setting time so we have a little more leeway in handling it we add a little liquid gelatin. This will slow up the setting time as much as an hour and is used when one models directly in plaster; and one which is much preferred by some professional casters, is to add beer.

"By now our cast should be ready to be removed from the mold. However, as this is a waste mold, we remove the mold from the cast. In this process the mold is destroyed and that is the derivation of the name. Also, that is the reason we made the mold of a different color from the cast, so in our process of chipping and prying to remove the mold, or pieces of it, we can readily discern one from the other and prevent damaging the cast.

"I want to call attention to one more item which is no less important than any of the rest of which I have spoken; this is to clean up your utensils and working area, and remove the waste. To do this while the plaster is fresh and not set is easy, but very difficult if left until the plaster has hardened.

"With this our demonstration is completed. I have given you an example of plaster casting in its most elementary form. From here the process extends in many directions, and it takes years of experience to understand all of its ramifications."

Dean Lawrence, I am happy to say, remained to the end, and the students were delighted and all had a permanent piece of their work.

The demonstration had the effect of popularizing the sculpture classes even more, and a student who wished to have a reproduction of his work could do so with a nominal charge for the plaster used. The money thus procured was carefully recorded and kept until a sufficient amount had been collected at which time a party was held in the studio for the entire group, and the money used to buy the refreshments of ice cream, cake and punch.

Another idea was developing in my mind. One of the entrances to the studio was through a small room used as a student locker room. It required only putting the lockers in another room to put my plan into effect.

Thus, we developed a small gallery for display of the students' work. In this way more incentive was added to give the students increased interest and ambition to excel. Only the most meritorius work was placed in the gallery and a keen competition developed in the classes. Before long we had a sizable exhibit of sculpture. The room was always lighted and the exhibit stimulated pride and interest in the department for outsiders were constantly coming in to visit and inspect the work. The students were encouraged and some of them occasionally sold a piece.

Practically all of my students showed outstanding talent and potential and deserved the high grades which were the norm in my department.

As the session was coming to a close I planned a party for the students. I had one particular surprise for them for which I prepared with the help of one of the students who happily turned out to have worked for a baker at one time. The surprise consisted of an ornately frosted birthday cake made of clay. Each slice had been cut and a prize inserted. Then the whole was assembled and frosted with a fancy plaster icing.

My wife and both children functioned as waiters for the occasion. When the cake was served, the guests were impressed by the size and ornate decoration, but a little concerened about eating it. Our dear old school superintendent, more courageous than the rest lifted a piece to his lips but was prevented from putting it in his mouth, thereby revealing the deception amid lots of laughter, and the added surprise of finding the gifts in the slices. There was ample real cake to satisfy everyone.

My teaching method was to see that there was never a dull moment with an equal balance between work and play. I was aided in this procedure by my students who enjoyed the easy informality, and they were motivated to work hard, and they all accomplished a great deal.

I was happy to note with the opening of the new term all of my students who had not graduated, were again registered in my classes, and a large new group joined us.

I was also pleased to receive another commission from Dean Lawrence, for a group of three figures, ultimately to be carved in stone and to stand in front of the Warner Oriental Art Museum to make a striking entrance.

We had collected a nice little sum from the charge for plaster, and I conferred with the students about a party to open the fall term.

The party was held in the courtyard of the Art and Architecture Building which had a cloistered walk all around it, and a balcony at the second floor of the two-story building. The courtyard was a perfect place for a party, and a very festive setting. A number of students modeled candelabras for the tables. There was entertainment by the students, including a Romeo and Juliet comedy scene utilizing the balcony. Students from the music department joined us and sang from opposite sides of the balcony, and a number of "telegrams" were read. One purportedly from the then President, Herbert Hoover, another from Oregon Governor Meyer, both expressing regret over their inability to attend such an important function. We even had a wrestling match between a very tall young man and a very short one, and after some hilarious antics, the little man won with everyone cheering.

I had invited Dean Lawrence and the faculty of the Art and Architecture Department, and Dean Lawrence said he was especially pleased because when he designed the building he had visualized the courtyard would be used for something like this.

My studio was the busiest place on campus. There were always students working on something. Some of them asked permission to model book-ends, so I had the whole class work upon this project and showed them what they could do. I was delighted with the results for they produced a wonderful assortment, showing great imagination. They naturally wanted to make casts, so I took the opportunity to teach them another casting technique: to make a gelatin mold for duplication.

The Life class showed great progress for they had the added advantage of having me work in the room with them. I knew from my own experience that students will watch the one who is best in the class, so it was a benefit for them to watch me.

We were fortunate in all of the art departments in being able to use nude models without being molested with all sorts of restricting rules and regulations by the administration.

One thing I required of the students from the very beginning of the classes was that the modeling tools they used be of the best quality and not the usual type to be purchased at the University book store which were little better than tooth-picks, being only about four inches long and poorly shaped. Not only was the expense very little more, but the balance and handling of the tool was distinctly helpful in the result. The obstacles for students to surmount are difficult enough without having to work constantly with unwieldly and poorly constructed tools. I was fortunate in finding a Mr. King who was a cabinet maker and wood carver, who made the tools for us. He used several of my own tools as models and did an excellent job.

There was another local craftsman, a Mr. Eckhard who was a furrier by trade. He had a very interesting private museum, mainly Indian artifacts and weapons of great rarity and beauty. His shop was a stopping place for "Travelers of the Road." When they were on their way through town they could pick up some change from him in exchange for the many rare items they had picked up on their journeys. They also whiled away the time making various handicraft items, a number of them were letter openers carved from bone which were exquisitely done. One of his prize pieces was a masterpice, an Eskimo harpoon carved from walrus ivory. The workmanship was unbelieveably fine. I availed myself of his collection and borrowed pieces to illustrate some of my lectures. I hoped the University would acquire this unique collection.

Mrs. Warner, the donor of the Oriental art collection to the university came to see me at my studio. She asked me to come to the museum as there was an object which needed a little repair work and she would like to have me do it for her. I acquiesced, and found that the repairs were insignificant, and I told her I would be glad to do it and there would be no charge.

The building was far from ready to open, but the displays were being put in place, and Mrs. Warner took me from case to case showing me the displays, pointing out objects throughout the building, and item after item was in need of repair, much of it of major proportion. She wanted me to repair all of them.

Unfortunately we never discussed the amount of work or the time involved. The following are some of the items as I remember them: a painted and carved wood Buddha, which took several days to repair; a number of Chinese terra cotta horses which were badly damaged and could not be displayed without major repair; teakwood screens with pictorial reliefs of jade from which fragments had been lost. To repair that I used white wax which I tinted to resemble jade. Also various pieces of furniture and innumerable other objects, including building tiles.

To make these various repairs required some ingenious substitution of materials, and took two months of my time, never working less than two hours a day. It was a challenge and I must say I throughly enjoyed it. After all was completed I sent Mrs Warner a bill for eight hundred dollars which I considered very modest.

She answered, reminding me that I had said I would not make a charge, completely forgetting that had been for the one small piece she

University studio with model of group for entrance to Warner Museum of Oriental Art

first showed me. She also said I had done the entire work of my own free will and could have stopped at any time; and that we had not made a contract so she owed me nothing.

I was surprised at her lack of consideration and appreciation for my work, and I decided to see an attorney and explained the case to him. His reaction was to say "Brother, you stepped into a bear trap, and the only thing you can do is forget it, for she is well-known for such conduct." I also spoke to the Dean about it, and he said "Your troubles are nothing to what I had to endure in the construction of the building for her collection." I later met a nephew of hers, and he laughed heartily when I related my experience, and exclaimed "That's Auntie all right."

The working model for the group of figures which were to stand at the entrance to the Oriental Art Museum was finished. This group of five foot high figures represented Life; the central figure holding a flower bud in her hands. There was a woman and child on the right, and on the other side an old man. The group was done in my angular style. They were to be carved in native stone, standing twice as high as my half life-size working model.[26]

One of my students, named Gardner, was an architecture major and a very ingenius fellow. He belonged to a fraternity which had just completed construction of its house near the campus. He conceived the idea of presenting the fraternity with a plaque of its crest, which he would make in the sculpture class in which he was registered. He started modeling the crest with great deliberation, receiving criticism from me. This he appreciated to the extent that, since I was doing so well he permitted me the privilege of finishing it, which I did, casting it as well. I was not fooled by his little deception but I knew too well a student's limitation and knew he had taken on a task he could not complete without help. He invited Mrs. Bock and me to attend the presentation.

Mr. Gardner, through his ambition and pursuasive talents managed another coup, by selling the idea to his architecture class to invite Frank Lloyd Wright to come to Eugene and give several lectures with an exhibition of his work. The wonder was that he was able to pull it off, apparently without help from the faculty, and an invitation was dispatched to Mr. Wright.[27]

It seems there was a considerable amount of correspondence before everything was arranged because they had only invited Mr. Wright, but I learned from him that he told them he would not come unless his wife, Olgivanna, was also invited and her expenses paid, as well as his.

Mr. and Mrs. Wright arrived in Eugene at about noon, registered at the Osborne Hotel and gave word he was not to be disturbed as he needed to rest from the trip. We spoke on the phone, and there was a reception for him that evening at the Music Building. He seemed tired and gave a little talk to the assembled guests and then retired.

There had been no special arrangements made by the faculty prior to his arrival, and Mr. Gardner was in despair over what he considered a slight, and he asked me what he should do, I told him we had planned to have Mr. and Mrs. Wright at our apartment for dinner the next evening, but as both our space and facilities were exceedingly limited it would be impossible to invite anyone else for dinner. However, after dinner we would hold an open house when anyone who wished could drop by and meet Mr. Wright informally.

Both Frank and Mr. Gardner were pleased with this plan, but the faculty seemed to feel they were being left out even though they had made no effort to arrange a social affair for him. However, a most enjoyable time was had, and after dinner the house was filled with students and others who came to meet the master.

The next day he gave a lecture to the students of the School of Architecture and Allied Arts, and Mr. Wilcox, head of the Architecture

Department, took Mr. Wright on a drive around Eugene and the campus. On the tour of the campus he was impressed with the appearance and modern design of the Warner Museum of Oriental Art, especially mentioning it, until he was told that what he was looking at was the back of the building where no attempt at design had been made.

That evening a banquet was held in the Mens' Dormitory by the Architectural Association for Mr. Wright and other honored guests. The speeches culminated in a very interesting debate between Wright, upholding the modern school of art, and the Architectural Assocation members speaking for the traditional. Frank always had a very caustic wit, and he accused them of being like the "Flu-Flu bird which always flew backward, for it was only interested in where it had been, and didn't care where it was going."

The evening included a series of stunts and sketches put on by the students, and were really ingenious. Rex Sorenson, one of my students, did an impression of me supposedly doing a lightning speed modeling of a head in five minutes. Upon a modeling stand he had a large lump of clay under which was a plaster bust painted the color of the clay. As he pretended to model he was removing the clay until finally the finished head was revealed to the amazement of everyone.

The painters, not to be outdone by the sculptors, staged a similar stunt. They had prepared a canvas with the head of a monkey painted in oil. When dry, the painting was covered over with a layer of tempera water color. In putting on the act, the artist announced he was going to attempt the almost impossible, to reveal the soul of man in his portrait. He had a model pose and then, with a number of brushes and small tins filled with water fastened to his pallet He painted with impressive flourishes and gestures. But rather than applying pigments, he was actually removing the water color coating from the oil painting, and finally revealed the head of the monkey. These stunts were clever and the applause was deserved.

The exhibit Wright brought to the campus consisted of drawings and some models which made quite an impression upon the students. Unfortunately, some of the conservative faculty seemed to feel threatened by Wright's non-conformist opinions, and were not enthusiastic about his visit. A few considered I was instrumental in bringing him to the campus and never really forgave me.

Before he left, I arranged a luncheon at the Anchorage so the students could have an informal visit with him. He enjoyed it and the students were really stimulated.

The next day Mr. and Mrs. Wright left for Portland and return to the east. Their visit had been an enriching experience for the students, and I was happy to see him again.[28]

Chapter XVIII
1932-1933

My sculpture classes were at their peak of achievement. The modeling class was working upon plaques, using as models, plates of the finest examples of modern architectural design, many I had gotten from the Chicago Art Institute. The classwork was filling our small museum with work which everyone viewed with pride.

The Dean came to my studio one day and informed me that I was over the retirement age, and he was very complimentary of my accomplishment in the department but said he could not continue me for the fall term. I was angered by the inflexible rules, the fear of tenure and the large part politics play. I naively thought a university would be above such rules. I hated to see my work with the students end, and with that feeling I made an impulsive offer to the Dean, to teach the sculpture classes for nothing, which startled the poor man so he exclaimed "You can't afford to do that." I said, however, I could for I had made up my mind to stay in Eugene for at least two more years, for it was the most inexpensive place to live during the deep depression years, and I wanted to complete a number of works I had started for a touring exhibition I had planned.

I liked the Dean very much, and I believe he liked me, but academic convention and conformity were too strong. Beside it might set a precedent.[29]

We stayed in Eugene another year and a half in the circle of my family, doing pieces of sculpture for my planned exhibition. Actually it was a very productive period for I was far from the center of art activity and I accomplished many pieces I might not have had time to do if I had been involved with commissions.

I regretted changes which were soon made in the sculpture department. The museum, the pride of the students and a strong incentive, had every vestige removed. Some of the students recovered their works from the university dump where they had been discarded. The new professor acquired some soft sandstone which is very easy to carve, from which the class created immediate art with no possibility to correct or change. I find it strange that some who have modest training prefer to work in permanent materials.[30]

When the dedication of the Campbell Court took place at the Warner Museum of Oriental Art at the end of my tenure at the University, Dean Lawrence asked me especially to be present so I could receive his appreciation for the work which I had done. I did so, and he was unstinting in his acknowledgement and praise, mentioning each individual panel and part of the work.

During the additional year we spent in Eugene, my son and daughter

A Campbell Court Lunette

continued to attend classes. Thor completed his art courses and received his Bachelor's Degree in Art. He later attended the University of Southern California in Los Angeles, where he received his Master's Degree and completed work toward his Doctor's.

The University Faculty Club chose "The Begger's Opera" for its yearly production, and asked my daughter to direct it, and my son to design and paint the scenery. Both received praise for their work.

As long as I was in Eugene I received calls from my students who came to me for aid and advice.

It was glorious living in a bounteous countryside, for I was working upon my models as I visualized having a traveling exhibition. This continued to be only a happy hallucination, for the country was in the throes of the worse depression in its history. So, I just continued to dream about my show, unaffected by the distressing conditions of the time. My life was one of tranquility, like a never ending vacation.

The house we lived in we rented from a Mrs. Riggs, which we later learned had at one time been occupied by two of the Pacific Northwest's most notorious train robbers. It was plain and unpretentious, but suited our purposes perfectly.

This "castle" of ours was situated on a small hill with a very high hill rising behind it. Along one side and cutting across the back of the house was a ravine. I must note that one of the great charms of this part of the country is that there are little streams everywhere. The front of the house was two stories while the back was three, where the entrance to the garage faced a small meadow and the ravine. The garage with its wood-burning furnace served as my workshop.

My family cooperated in every respect to my needs. There was a small room which served as a museum for my completed works, and also a study with the entire north wall of glass which served as my studio. There remained on the first floor the living-room, dining-room and kitchen. The second floor was devoted to bedrooms and bath. All of the rooms were of ample size but it was the outside that most intrigued us. At the garage door there was a drive coming down from the street with a low brick wall at one side. It was in this protected area where, when the weather was good, we usually had our lunch with a view of the ravine which was overhung with a tangle of wild blackberry vines. From here the sloping mountain meadow, carpeted with wild flowers rose steeply, its sides covered with evergreen and deciduous trees. This was the idealic view which delighted our eyes while we lingered over lunch, and our daughter read a portion of a chosen book to us.

Within an hour's walk from our house in any direction was a virtually untouchd wilderness in which all forms of wild life abounded, including deer, bear and mountain lions. With these near neighbors we avoided any dispute over territorial rights, and they did not encroach upon Eugene's highways.

During the winter season it was necessary to keep a fire burning. Almost everyone burned wood in their stoves and furnaces.[31] The wood was pine which burns with a terrific heat. Practically every house had a great stack of wood beside it, and it didn't seem to matter how wet it got from the rain because of the resin and pitch, but it created a great deal of soot which necessitated a chimney cleaning every fall.

There was one chimney cleaner in Eugene who was quite a character. He looked just like the old world Chimney Sweeps, right out of Dickens. He walked around town with the implements of his trade slung over his shoulder, and upon his head he wore a tall silk opera hat with a sign across the front proclaiming his profession. All the time he was working, standing upon the roof tops, he would sing loudly, in quite a good voice. He was a favorite, especially with the fraternity and sorority houses which hired him as much for the entertainment as for the services rendered.

Portraits of Phoenix Kang, Agnes Petzold and Billy Rivers

After I left the University I had an exhibition of some of my work in Portland, which lasted two weeks. Most of the works I exhibited were portrait busts. The show was very well accepted and I received excellent notices in all of the newspapers. I stayed in the city during the exhibit, and I enjoyed a reunion with some of my former students who lived in the vicinity. They entertained me and took me on several short trips, one of which was a drive along the magnificent Columbia River Gorge, a breath-taking view of one of the great beauties of nature. Another interesting experience was to see the annual run of smelt, a small silvery fish. They were packed into the river in such tremendous numbers that it seemed impossible for water to flow past them. During the short period of their run people would wade into the river with pails, bushel baskets or anything which came to hand to scoop the fish from the water. Humans lined the banks almost as thickly as the fish jammed the water. Literally millions of smelt were caught in a few hours.

Another time I exhibited a portrait head of a young girl with the Portland Society of Artists exhibit, which was held in a new gallery. My entry won first prize in the sculpture division.

Sundays we reserved for worshipping God and all nature. With the aid of my son's trusty car, we drove anywhere our heart's desired, usually into the distant forests.

Naturally, one of the most important parts of these jaunts was the picnic lunch we took with us. Our favorite was small rib steaks prepared in a special way we called "Oregon Steaks." Wherever you go in this beautiful country you are near a stream, and after choosing a spot for our picnic we gathered wood for a fire, and flat rocks about ten or twelve inches wide, worn smooth in the rushing stream. The rocks were put in the fire and allowed to remain until they were very hot. After the blaze had died down a little and the rocks were hot, they were pulled from the fire and quickly rubbed with a piece of bacon which both cleaned and greased the surface. Then a thin rib steak was placed on the rock. They cooked very quickly. Steaks cooked this way are delicious and very tender. For some reason the toughest steaks become tender. Naturally we brought all other picnic items including ice cream packed in dry ice that we picked up at the fruit packing plant in Eugene.

One of our favorite picnic locations was an old abandoned mill, deep in the forest on the side of a mountain. We had to leave the car at a farm at the bottom of the hill and walk up a corduroy road, which is a roadway

"The Cloud"

made of logs laid close together, and very difficult to walk upon. It paralleled the ruins of the flume which was used to transport the cut logs down the mountainside.

At the mill which had been abandoned for many years, the buildings still stood in a very dilapidated condition with most of the rusted heavy equipment still in place. It was always very quiet and there was an aura of mystery. There was the remains of the mill pond, and this is where we held our picnics. Sitting quietly at dusk we saw many forms of wild life who came to drink. One time we were held at bay by a skunk who decided to walk down the corduroy road the same time we were leaving. He refused to yield the right of way, and as we did not care to argue with him, we ambled slowly at a discrete distance behind him almost the entire distance down the hill. Another time our daughter was chased down the hill by a cow that apparently wanted to be milked.

Another location that gave us much pleasure was far up the north fork of the McKenzie River. To get there we had to drive through a deep forest, at one point over a dam, and we always stopped to watch the huge salmon fighting their way up the fish ladders in their effort to get past the dam and up stream to their spawning grounds. We never tired of the abundant vegetation everywhere, even finding tiny orchids growing out of the moss on tree trunks.

While the country was trying to extricate itself from the Depression,

I was busy building dream castles. One of my plans was a colossus for the harbor of Los Angeles, a statue built of rustless steel to be for the West Coast what the Statue of Liberty is for the East Coast. Another of my brain children of colossal proportions was, also, to be built in the South West. It was to be a statue three hundred feet high, to represent an Indian seated on the ground, wrapped in a blanket. The interior was to serve as an Indian museum to be erected of local material, especially the lava stone which abounds in parts of the South West, the statue was to rest upon a square base about twenty feet high, to serve as a plinth to house the museum. This base was to be carved with a running relief of Indians, depicting their history and activities. The backs of their war bonnets were to contain the cathedral windows to the interior.

I had always had a desire to see the world's oldest living things, the giant Redwoods and Sequoias of Northern California, so one summer we took a vacation trip through this territory. I was not disappointed in my expectations, for they are an awesome and never to be forgotten sight. In leaving Oregon we drove from Grants pass to Crescent City on the coast in California. The road followed Nichols Creek almost all of the way. This enchanting mountain stream tumbles over its rocky bed of varicolored stones, the water colored a strong blue-green from dissolved minerals.

From Crescent City we followed the Redwood Highway through forests of these giant trees, always marvelling at their size and age, as well as their beauty, and the luxuriance of the woodland carpet which surrounds them with a dense growth of underbrush and large ferns.

It saddened us to pass through an area which had just suffered the ravages of a forest fire, so recent that the charred remains of trees and brush were still smoking. Now and then the quick licking of flames could be seen. The entire area was densely covered with a pall of smoke, and firefighters were still standing by with their equipment against the possibility of the fire breaking out again.

From there we were soon in the even more majestic and awe-inspiring forest of the "Big Trees," the Sequoias, which had looked out over the surrounding countryside in their serenity since before the coming of the Ice Age whose glaciers miraculously passed them by. We stayed overnight in this park in order to commune with their spirits. One has a feeling of being in a cathedral; you unconsciously lower your voice, and your footsteps are soundless on the deep carpet underfoot. Mankind and his troubles seem so insignificant and transient. Who would ever again be impressed with his own importance after seeing and being overawed by these trees and their history, so nearly indestructible that fires, floods, storms and the passing years are but a phase in their lives? Only man has had the ability to destroy these monuments to the past, so legislation had to be passed to protect them from the one enemy capable of bringing about their destruction.

Greatly uplifted and refreshed, we continued our trip and visited Monterey, the first capital of California with all of its places of historic interest and artistic beauty. We also paid a visit to Carmel, the famous

Model for a Fountain for Portland, Oregon

artists' colony, in its lovely setting overlooking the ocean. So, on to Los Angeles and a pleasant stay of a few weeks.

On our return trip to Oregon we took the central route in order to save both time which was getting short, and to observe new scenery. We had a distant view of Mount Lassen, the only active volcano in the mainland United States. Looking at it through a telescope we could see a faint curl of smoke rising from its crater, a reminder that it is only slumbering, and stirs occasionally in its sleep.

We passed Mount Shasta, just at dawn, and saw another never to be forgotten sight. A magnificent sunrise coming up over a distant range of mountains threw a brilliant back light upon this beautiful snow-covered peak, coloring it a light pink. As evidence of the terrific winds blowing around its crest, a long plume of snow stretched out from its snow cap, sparkling and glittering in the rays of the sun, tinting it with the reflected light of all the other sunrise colors while the base of the mountain was still held in deep shadow.

We had intended to take the side trip to see Crater Lake in Oregon, but it was imperative that we be in Eugene the next day, so we had to bypass this famous extinct volcano with its deep blue lake which rests in its crater.

During our four year stay in this garden spot I accomplished a great deal of work, including a large amount of writing. In my connection with the University, I realized that there was a great need for a book on sculpture, especially of its various techniques. As there was no comprehensive book on the subject, and no one knew the subject more fully than I, I decided to rectify the lack, and started a comprehensive work which I continued working on after I returned to Chicago, when I also wrote an accompanying book on anatomy. Both of these works are fully illustrated, but at the present time they are still in manuscript form.[32] I also wrote a number of children's stories and an epic poem on the serpent, its place in history and art.

Among the exhibition pieces I worked on during this period was one I called "Voices of the Wind" which depicts souls in distress, suggested to me by the moaning and sighing of the wind. The first section of this composition I called "Earth Bound," showing two figures, a man and a woman. The man showed a back view, seated on a mound of earth, and in a very strained position. To his left was the female figure seated on the ground below him with the man's head resting upon her left shoulder, her hand in his hair as if steadying him in his deep emotion. Her right hand digging into earth as she weeps in anguish. There are numerous other figures in this composition, one, a woman with streaming hair groping along a wall, I call "Without a Friend." Another part is a reclining figure which I call "Abandoned." There were two other parts planned to complete the cycle, representing "Infancy" and "Music" which I have never worked upon so the composition remains incomplete.

This was undoubtedly my most concentrated, uninterrupted productive period. I worked steadily and happily. Other pieces which I completed in Oregon for my private exhibition for which some of my students posed, as did my wife and children, were "Perseus" and "Andromeda," half life-size nudes, and a very unusual composition; a

"EarthBound"

standing figure of Moses, half life-size and done in my angular style, which I planned to carve in wood; a small nude girl with a shell, called "Whispers;" a large angular reclining figure, a composition which is my interpretation of Wagner's "Rhinegold;" a seated figure representing "Fate;" a number of smaller pieces including a very strong, abstract composition of Pan; a number of portrait busts including my daughter, and an unusal composition of my son, as well as an elfin head called "Sprite" suggested by a piece of candle wax Dorathi had been moulding in her fingers.

There was also a group called "Hagar and Ishmael;" a stocky nude female called "Susana at the Bath;" a small statue of Mercury; another small statue of the runner Arthur Holman, in a very realistic and accurate pose of a runner in action; an eighteen inch standing draped figure with upraised arms as in prayer, for which my daughter posed and called "A Dancer;" another statuette of a similar figure, undraped; another nude figure, called "The Grape;" two nude seated figures in classic style, and a small statuette entitled "Beauty and the Beast."

At this time I also completed a favorite piece of work. One moonlit summer night, before we were married, my sweetheart and I were seated in a secluded spot watching the fleecy clouds drifting across the face of the moon, forming fantastic patterns. One such shape suggested the shape of a recumbant woman, a perfect form for sculpture. Remembering this design, the next morning I started work on a sketch using this inspiration. I visualized it as a perfect representation of woman, embodying her changeability, keeping one between ecstacy and doubt, in laughter and tears, and both helpful and sacrificing, gentle and violent like a tempest, truly an enigma.

Owing to a great deal of work I had at that time, I was prevented from starting this piece until several years later, after I had been married to this heavenly apparition, when she posed for it. The work was completed and put on exhibition when it received commendation from the critics, but it was a disappointment to me, and for some thirty years this piece went through a number of changes, through all of my art periods. Eventually it was completed while I was in Oregon. However, in this last stage it has never been exhibited., and I fear for its destiny.

I fear oblivion may be the fate of all my private exhibition work. I have in mind to give it to a representative art museum if I were assured of its security. In the absence of this, I have considered destroying it all, for I know only too well that the great museums are not above spoilation, for I have been in the basement of the Chicago Art Institute many times, which is fittingly called "The Morgue." It is packed to capacity with fine work, paintings, and marble and bronze sculptures. Most of it will never be exhibited. Every new director of a museum, in his course, makes his contribution to these morgues, removing works from the main galleries to make room for something new, or more to his personal taste, representing the style of the moment, of the school in which he trained, or the taste of a wealthy donor who has made an endowment to the institution.

Chapter XIX
1934-1946

It was now time for us to think about leaving our haven in Eugene and return home after having been away for over four years.

Our preparations for departure required a great amount of effort, for nearly all my works were in plaster and had to be individually crated in such a manner as to preclude any possibility of being broken in transit, as I still hoped to have a travelling exhibition. My son and I made individual crates to fit all of the larger pieces; the smaller ones, after being well padded and wrapped, were placed in large boxes, all of which had to be numbered and contents listed.

Eventually the crating was completed and I had all of the boxes put in storage until arrangement could be made for them to be shipped elsewhere.

All that remained then was the closing of our household. We sold all of the furniture we had purchased to second-hand furniture dealers. My son now had a Cadillac in place of his trusty old Chandler. We bought a two-wheel trailer, loaded it down with all of our trunks and personal effects which made a very heavy load, and were ready to depart for Los Angeles.

We spent our last night in Eugene under rather primitive conditions, as all of the furniture had been removed from the house, and at dawn the next day we were up and on our way with real regret at leaving Oregon where we had been so happy.[33]

For a number of miles we were apprehensive about the trailer turning over as the heavy load made it sway as turns were made on the winding mountain roads. However, it had been well balanced and the center of gravity was low, so we soon lost our fear and hurried on our way.

We arrived at the California Border Control Station where cars are searched in an effort to prevent destructive insect pests and plant diseases from entering the State. The personnel were both efficient and courteous and gave us no trouble with our heavy load.[34]

Among the things we had packed as being indispensible, were half a dozen of the round, flat river stones, so we could have Oregon picnics when we got home.

We stopped at Yreka, an interesting mining town just below the Oregon border, the first good-sized city in California as you enter the state on the inland route from the north. We had dinner and decided to spend the night and get an early start in the morning.

From the time we descended the mountains of Northern California we traversed the flat stretch of road through the central valley, often called America's Salad Bowl for its miles of commercial produce acreage. The sun was bright and the heat intense, and it seemed each fence post had a bird resting in its shade. From Bakersfield south to the steep climb called the Grapevine Grade, the road is perfectly straight for miles, and people often go to sleep because of the monotony of driving, causing serious

"A Dancer"

"Whispers"

accidents. We passed several cars at roadside with people resting. The Ridge Route crosses the mountain into Los Angeles, and is a beautiful stretch of bare hills so different from the tree shrouded hills of Oregon, but just as beautiful in their stark play of light and shadow.

We finally arrived at our destination, a nice little furnished bungalow in Hollywood, which our son-in-law had rented for our sojourn. He had a delicious dinner prepared for us, and with the comforts of the little house, it was a delightful welcome.

Mrs. Bock and I stayed in Hollywood, resting and enjoying the climate and surrounding countryside for a month. We wanted to get back to Chicago in time to see the Century of Progress Exposition, so we finally made our train reservations and said reluctant farewells to our family who were remaining in California.

We arrived in Chicago just in time to attend the last day of the Exposition on November 2, 1934. The enormous crowds on this last day degenerated into a wrecking crew, destroying everything they could get their hands on, and taking souvenirs. We felt fortunate to get out without incident for many people were injured.

Two of the exhibits, one a village in old England, and the other a village in New England with Paul Revere's silver shop, were picturesque and beautifully created.

I have participated in three World's Fairs, all of them outstanding, and of extravagant artistic design. Of them all the Chicago Columbian

Exposition of 1893 was the finest in artistic achievement with its classical architecture and statuary. I have no criticism to make of the past expositions; they were all artistically excellent. The San Francisco Exposition was possibly more artistically fanciful and was the last to display abundant statuary. The Palace of Fine Arts by the architect Maybeck was an outstanding architectural triumph.

Therefore, when I beheld this last Chicago Exposition, it was a disappointment when I could not find a single piece of sculpture. There was only one sculptural feature, a gigantic bas relief of a single figure with a serpent in a pretzel-like coil. What had become of art?

It seemed that the trend was toward a lavish use of color and electrical lighting displays, coupled with large plain masses of architectural form with a few pieces of sculpture handled in the Moderne Style, which to me is not as pleasant as the classic style used in previous expositions.

The New York Century of Progress went wild with the Moderne in which the Trianon and Perisphere could not save it from monotony.

Mrs. Bock and I stayed overnight at the Congress Hotel, and the next day we were back once again in our home in River Forest, which had been rented during our long absence by Mr. and Mrs. Frederick Basatt.

It was a strange world I came back to after a four year absence. "Out of sight, Out of mind," and there were no commissions except those which were being dispensed by the WPA, and in which I never participated, feeling the entire setup was based entirely upon politics instead of art. I must say, however, that the program in general accomplished a great deal of good in the many projects which were done for the public welfare, although there were also some which accomplished nothing aside from being the payment of a dole which, being part of the plan, I suppose you might say fulfilled its purpose. Although the quality was not always of the finest, much was gained in popularizing art, not only by the WPA but also by the Procurement Division of the Public Building Program which constructed Federal Buildings such as Post Offices for which competitions were held for murals to be painted on the walls. The winners of these competitions were given contracts, and the public gained in the way of some fine mural painting, though there were many whose excellence was questionable.

A new phase of art I dare say will not leave a very lasting imprint, its disciples choose to call "Interpretive," and under this head almost anything is called art, including the most absurd contradictions. The artists, many with no art training, simply express themselves with absurdities.

As for myself and my posterity, I have never suffered for I was one of the first, some have said the first, to express myself in an interpretive, abstract way, but always with my work firmly grounded in basic technical knowledge. There is always a logical limit for any art, and it must have harmony as its goal, and it must exalt the spirit. It is not art if it does not make sense. Pure abstraction can be very beautiful, but it must be based upon harmony, harmony of both technique and imagination.

The handcrafts of primitives show an harmonious excellence. They always fashioned and decorated their implements with some of the most

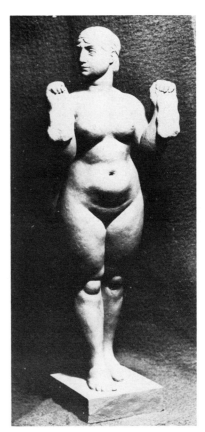

"Susana at the bath"

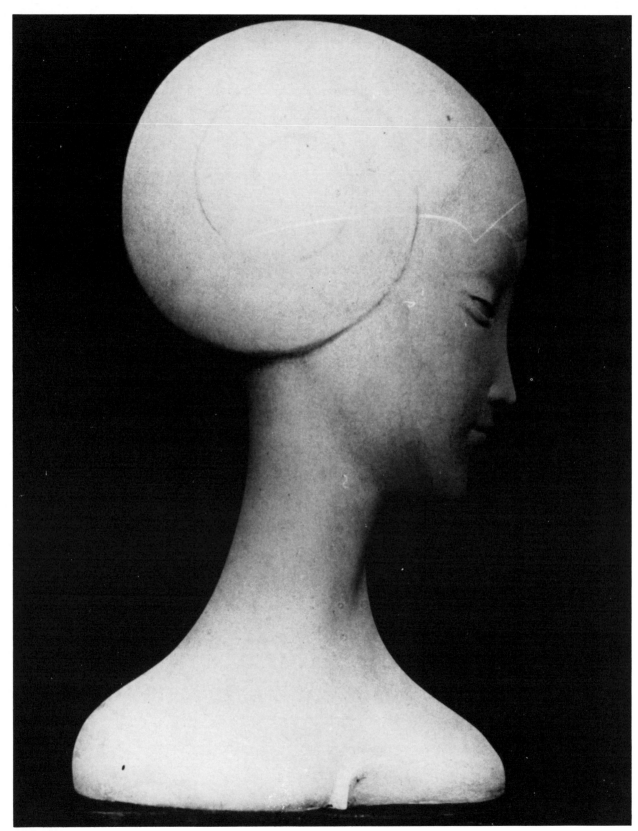

"Sprite"

exquisite pure forms of art, some of it abstract, using an inordinate amount of creative effort.

In art, civilized man has followed the same steps as his forebears down through the centuries as may be seen in the work created by the Egyptians, Assyrians and through chronological order all of the ancient civilizations. The beauty of their art, created with only the most primitive tools, judging from our standards, is awesome and an accomplishment of the greatest magnitude. Their craftsmanship still fascinates us and commands our admiration today as it has in the past and will continue to do so.

I received one more large commission, from Michael Pontarelli. This work was for his family mausoleum. It comprised two figures of angels in marble, also two portrait busts, of Mr. and Mrs. Pontarelli. These were to be done in Carrara marble.

I was unable to find a pointer carver in the city of Chicago, so I wrote to several of my friends in New York asking them to refer me to a dependable carver. Hermon MacNeil, commenting in his note to me, asked "How in the world are you able to get marble portraits to do in these days?" He referred me to Arthur Lorenzani, to whom I entrusted the work of copying my models, and I was very satisfied with his work.

I also did a bronze drinking fountain for Ann Arbor, Michigan, to be placed on the University of Michigan campus; and two horses' heads I carved in wood for the Babson Stables in Riverside, Illinois.

Our friends Wilma and Fred Basatt, had occupied our stuido during our absence in Oregon, and enjoyed living there. The freedom and artistic character of the studio, surrounded by big trees and dense underbrush, pleased them very much. Fred was employed in the laboratory of the American Can Company in Maywood, and we saw them often after our return. He was being transfered to New York, and before leaving he said he had a favor to ask of me. Knowing of my close friendship with Frank Lloyd Wright, he wondered if I could get an invitation for him and his wife and Mrs. Bock and me to visit Taliesin; if so he would drive us there. I have not mentioned before that I never learned to drive, and we did not have a car until my son was old enough to get a driver's license. The day after Fred's suggestion, I wrote to Frank, and received an immediate reply of welcome for the following weekend.

Fred asked me "By the way, does the great man know you so well that he will slap you on the back and call you Dickie, and then put his arm around you and chide you for never calling on him?"

Taliesin, Wright's studio in Spring Green, near Madison, Wisconsin, is nearly two hundred miles from Chicago, where he moved when he left his family in Oak Park. The property was left to him by two aunts who had operated a school there, and where he eventually established a fellowship of student architects.

We arrived at Taliesin about four o'clock in the afternoon one Saturday in early November. First, greeting us inside the entrance drive, and poised upon a high brick pedestal, was a terra cotta copy of my Dana House figure, the "Flower in the Crannied Wall." We did not stop, and after a turn or two and a stretch of wall with gourds growing over it, the view

"Moses"

137

"Perseus"

quite suddenly opened up to a spacious form of man's creative imagination. Here was the completed structure I was seeing for the first time. It was a self-portrait, not unlike a Rembrandt. The same adjectives apply to both men, for both were rugged individualists, firm in their own convictions: sensative, intimate, glamorous, each having a love of finery and of possessions, yet generous. This also applies equally to their work.

Someone had seen us coming up the drive and several young men came out of the house to meet us and show us where the car was to be parked. We entered the house and into a large room which was apparently used as a location for meetings and debates which Frank loved. As we entered a discussion was in progress with most of the young men standing at ease. As we were introduced to everyone in Wright's bouyant manner, he greeted me exactly as Fred, in his facetious imagination had questioned. As I cast a side glance toward Fred, he nodded and smiled.

We all moved over toward the fireplace and stood around in a group while light refreshments were served.

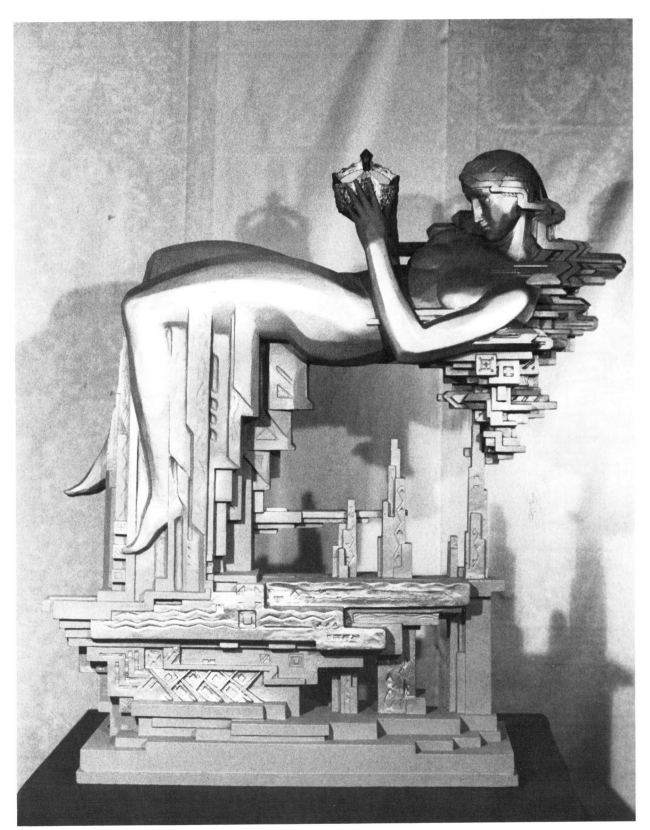

"Lure of the Rhinegold"

"Labor"

I had brought a small gift of a child's story I had written, and I asked Frank to read it to the young group before we were shown to our rooms. This he did with his usual flourish, and everyone liked it. He said, however, that as an adult's opinion and a child's differ considerably, he suggested that it be read by his little six year old daughter. This was done and she was enthusiastic about it, so I was happy.

We had a most enjoyable dinner, and a wine which Mrs. Wright had made from their own grapes. The food was delicious and our host set the manner of using his fingers in eating the chicken, saying "That is the way nature intended it to be done."

After dinner we went to his "Little Theater" to see a motion picture. The theater was formerly the Hillside School for Girls, which had been run by Frank's maiden aunts, Jane and Nell Lloyd Jones. He loved the theater as I did, and he had converted the school into a marvelous auditorium and theater with a fascinating artistic interior. Once a week a film is shown, which all the people in the vicinity may attend.

At the time of our visit there was still some construction work going on upon the main buildings although they were nearly completed. the school section, which contained a large drafting room was about seventy-five feet from the main house.

The whole structure was of stone, concrete and wood. I was particularly impressed with the massive oak beams supporting the ceilings, and their unique design. The materials were either quarried or felled by the students who finished the material themselves, or they took the logs to the mill to be sawed into boards. They then used this material as part of their class work to construct the buildings. The entire project was the result of the labors of Wright's students, who came to his school for the privilege of working under his tutelage, and as architects they learned how to use the materials of their profession.

I agree with his method as part of the learning process for artists should know the feel of their materials, not only by reading about them.

In a way it was similar to what Mrs. Bock and I did, constructing much of our home and studio ourselves, and thus getting a special enjoyment from it, for it not only grew with us but it also had a part of us built into it. It was a living thing, and that feeling was inherent in the development of our family life and our children who also contributed to the building, gathering rocks and boulders on our property from which we built our fireplace.

During our stay at Taliesin we were shown a huge celler which was stocked with the results of the boys enterprise in the truck gardens which produced bounteous crops. There were quantities of stored and canned vegetables, fruits and other farm produce. When Fred Basatt saw the canned goods he shuddered, for he was very suspicious of most of it and said that it would be dangerous to eat. He told Frank that through his connection with the can company he could get him a second-hand professional pressure canner at a great saving, which would alleviate the danger of food poisoning. Mrs. Wright was very proud of her quantities of preserves, a number of barrels of sauerkraut and numerous sacks of potatoes, and well she might be for it was no easy task to manage such an establishment, even with the help of many willing hands.

Sunday morning at breakfast it was decided to go on a picnic, about four or five cars of us. We went to a very beautiful spot on the banks of a little stream. It was a delightful day even though it was chilly. We returned from the picnic about four o'clock and had to leave almost immediatley for the long drive home. It was bitter cold on the return trip, and even with steady driving we did not reach River Forest until two o'clock in the morning.

In the manifold experiences in art, the Master of Taliesin stands preeminently alone as a living example of fundamental training. He has given more than he has taken from life's sweet treasures, and for that he has paid a heavy price. At this date, 1946, he is still doing creative work of the first magnitude.

I do not expect we will meet again.

"Andromeda"

Chapter XX
Afterthoughts

All of my life I have tried to invent something that would furnish me with a steady income which would support me so I could devote my entire energies to uninterrupted effort in achieving my highest goals in art, and I have belatedly come to the conclusion that I have no talent for business or finances.

My first idea was developed when I was twenty-one years old. It was a folding paper box which would lie flat for stacking when not in use. It had a string inserted all around near the top, starting from the center, with the other end coming out through the same hole. All that was required to make it a box was to pull on the two ends of the string which caused all sections to assume their proper position and the ends to be reinforced, while the string tied up the resultant box. It was perfect in action, and quite ingenious, but when I had it examined for a patent, it was discovered that an identical article had been invented in Germany five years before, and papers had been taken out in the United States. That was the loss of my first "million" and the ten dollars for the patent search.

At an even earlier age, when I was no more than sixteen, I played around with an automatic tack hammer which was similar to the present day stapler. This was in the days of wall-to-wall carpeting with its injuries to those who lay the carpet when they missed the tack but not the fingers. However, I was too young to develop this idea to the manufacturing stage, and I soon lost interest.

Another youthful idea I had was for a hospital stretcher which was not only collapsible, but could also be used as a bed. I received a patent for this and it was written up in various scientific journals. I received many requests and offers for it, but as I had an inflated idea of its value, I turned them all down, and finally I was left with my stretcher and no more offers.

I developed a novel idea for an attachment for a serving fork, so that by a simple pressure of the finger articles which had been impaled upon the fork would be forced off. This is another idea I let go by default.

Then there was a game for children. It was small and punched out of cardboard. It started out as a basketball game and a number were sold. However, the promoter who was handling the article made little effort so the project died a natural death. I later changed it to a Mayan Ring Ball game which improved it very much, but it never had any promotion. For this object I became interested in electroplating for I wished the game to be pressed. This led to another idea of making a very artistic and decorative top for a candy box. My problem with this was to find a light, durable, inexpensive and easily fabricated material which could be turned out in mass production. The process met all of the requirements except for the limitation of the quantity that could be turned out by one mold. This has never been pursued.[35]

In the course of my career I have done a considerable amount of decorative work for display purposes. At Christmas time there is always a great demand for fanciful ideas. I had a number of different sections of some decorative motifs lying around the studio, including a third section of a model for a full-size Christmas tree to be finished six feet high and lighted from the inside with the light to penetrate through innumerable openings scattered over the surface of the tree. These sections of the tree were to be fastened around the columns on the main floor of a department store. This full-size tree, however, was finally abandoned, leaving me with the preparatory model which was about a foot high. It was near Christmas time and my wife was thinking of planning something for our daughter in far-off California. Looking about, and seeing my sketch, she picked up three of the sections of the model and held them together, making a perfect, full-round tree. She asked me to fasten them together, insert an electric bulb in the base, and then we would have a perfect Christmas tree lamp. No sooner said than done, and the whole thing was perfect. We made the lamp of plaster, painted it green, touched it up with snow on its branches, put the light bulb in it and shipped it off to the children.

"Stagnation"

A gift shop convention was in progress in Chicago at this time so we made another tree and Mrs. Bock took it to the convention and put it on display in one of the booths. It made an instant hit for it was the one uniuqe article on display that year, and a great many orders were received. The only difficulty was the trees could not be made fast enough.

A salesman for the Illinois Candy Box Company saw it and said he would like to handle it, so we gave him a sample. In one week he sold to one concern alone, several thousand of the lamps which gave us a profit of over a thousand dollars. We had but this one salesman, and he sold so many trees in the United States and Hawaii that we were completely swamped with orders.

I made a contract with Carson Pirie Scott Department Store, and Mr. McDonald, head of the display art department was very interested and asked me if I had patented the tree. When I said no he advised me to do so immediately, and he even took me to a patent attorney who could not see that I had anything to patent but finally agreed that I did, and I eventually received a patent without any difficulty.

At last it seemed my dream of an invention which would bring me a steady income had come true. However, this was a bubble which was destined to burst due to my lack of business knowledge and ability. I could design, I could create, but I had no idea what to do after that.

With all of the sales appeal and the orders which continued to pour in, and the improvements I made in the article, it was still made of plaster and was heavy and fragile. Every step of the process of manufacture had to be done well, and there were too many parts and steps involved. The packing had to be carefully done and the shipping was heavy so the margin of profit was small. Of course, it could have been redesigned and

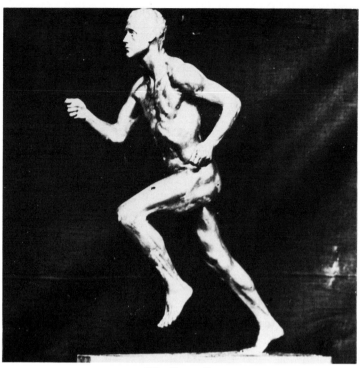

"The Runner"

made of a different material, and we could have had a company do the manufacture, but it had all happened too fast. After that first year I found it took too much time from my own work, and I just let it die. But it was this tree that was the parent of the swarm of trees that came after as copies in many different forms and materials, but none could equal ours.

In order to complete the record of the variety of my art experiences, I must mention some work I did in pottery.

When our children were quite small we had a family conference to decide upon a name for my studio. The name suggested by my son was the one finally decided upon, and the studio was known as "The Gnomes" from that time on, even serving as our mailing address.

Using the gnomes as a theme, I made a number of small sculptures down through the years, and then finally I decided to make a set of children's table china, using "Snow White and the Seven Dwarfs" as a subject. This was years before Walt Disney made his film of the fairytale.

This set consisted of a plate, cup and saucer, a porridge bowl, a small pitcher for cream, a covered sugar bowl and a napkin ring.

The plate and saucer were of conventional child's size and shape with incised relief. The plate showed the seven dwarfs marching along in a single file around the inside surface; the saucer showed, in the same style, the dwarfs' house in the center, and around the outer area all of the various animals and birds they met in the forest as they journeyed to and from their work. The colored glaze on these pieces filled in the incised and modeled areas bringing out the pattern and full modeling against a lighter background.

The porridge bowl was in the form of a cup-shaped flower, with the top edge rounded and smooth with three dwarfs at different points on the outside, with their fingers grasping the rim as they strain to peek over the top to see what is inside.

The cup was the same form as the porridge bowl, with the handle the young prince, his outstretched arms partially encircling the rim of the cup while his toes touch the base.

The sugar bowl was also of the flower form, with dwarfs at three equal points on the outside, with their backs to the bowl seeming to support the petals and keep its contents from overflowing. The lid had a small knob in the form of a witch's head with a pointed cap, while her swirling cloak formed the cover. The cream pitcher also had the flower form with the handle being formed by Snow White, her back to the pitcher as she grasps the edge with her hands in back of her head and her feet and dress attached to the bottom.

The last piece, the napkin ring, was formed by the kneeling figure of a huntsman, his arms outstretched in front of him and his hands holding the stock of an up-ended cross-bow which rests upon the ground in front of him, thus leaving an opening through which to insert the napkin.

The set is unusual and technically correct for reproduction. I am afraid, however, that it will remain only a display art object as there were only two sets made and the molds for the set have been lost.

I also made the designs for a number of salt and pepper shakers in various art forms, the molds for these have presumably also been lost.[36]

Richard W. Bock, 1947

Epilogue

After mother and father returned to River Forest in 1934, they did some remodeling on the studio, sold one of the adjacent lots, and father had several small commissions. A year or so later he noticed a physical weakness which developed slowly but was difficult for so active a man. In 1944 they came to California to spend the winter with us, and never returned to Chicago.

About the end of the War my husband had business in Chicago and I accompanied him. When we visited the studio we were shocked to find it had been burglarized and terribly vandalized. I spent three weeks cleaning out, packing and disposing of everything which had been left and not mutilated. These things were shipped to Los Angeles and put in storage, and later the collection in Oregon was brought to Los Angeles.

Father continued to write, including these memoirs in 1946, aided by my brother, though it became increasingly difficult, reaching the point when he could no longer hold a pencil, and tied it to his hand with a hankerchief. He became active in encouraging a movement to erect his Los Angeles colossus, which was not realized.

He died on June 29, 1949, just two weeks before his eighty-fourth birthday, from complications of advanced Parkinson's Disease.

We were a very close and loving family. Mother and father sometimes disagreed but never quarreled, and they were openly affectionate. I remember a fortune teller once told me "You come from a family that laughs together," and she was right.

Father was an irrepressible optimist. He could not remain angry or hold a grudge. He had a wonderful sense of humor, and a great zest for life.

Thor and I were very young when we moved into father's studio "until the Wright studio is built." It was a wonderful arrangement for children for we grew up in a heavily-wooded private world, in a close relationship with our parents, surrounded by art in an active art atmosphere. It was wonderful for father, too, because he would come to the door of his studio and call out "Mattie, can you get . . .?"or "Can you help me?" And whatever it was, she was always there and able to respond.

Mother was a beautiful woman and a natural artist of many talents. She had a beautiful speaking and singing voice; she made lovely pottery; she designed and made my dancing costumes; she was a genius in the garden, and she skinned, cured and mounted innumerable snake skins and various bugs and butterflies for the children who came to play in our wading pool. One time she even cured the skin of a mole that had been caught in a mouse trap, and she made a stole and muff from it for one of my many dolls.

Through the interest of Dr. Donald P. Hallmark, who wrote his Master's and Doctor's theses on the works of Richard W. Bock, the collection was brought to the attention of the Administration of Greenville College in Greenville, Illinois. They offered a permanent home to the entire collection of hundreds of items of sculpture, drawings, paintings and father's art library. The collection fills an historic Victorian house on the campus, named the Richard W. Bock Sculpture Museum, which was dedicated in 1975.

My one regret is that father did not live to know his collected works have been permanently preserved as he had hoped they would be.

I am personally grateful to Dr. Hallmark for his books on Richard W. Bock, and to those at Greenville College for their far-sighted and generous support: Dr. Orley Herron, President of Greenville College in 1972, and Dr. W. Richard Stephens, now President of the College, who has continued and broadened the dedicated preservation and support of the collection.

Dorathi Bock Pierre

Notes

#

1   (page 2)   In some of the early dates, there is a discrepancy between father's memory and Dr. Hallmark's research. For the sake of chronological accuracy where there is a doubt I have used Dr. Hallmark's finding.

2   (page 5)   Often one name is used, either a given or surname, and unfortunately, there is no reference source to complete or verify them.

3   (page 6)   Father always loved the theater. He had a very catholic taste, and we went to everything. I remember bits of plays and operas I saw when I was no more that three years old. Every major event in our family was either celebrated or mourned by attending a theater performance.

4   (page 18)   The Library was destroyed during World War I.

5   (page 18)   It was detroyed after the First World War.

6   (page 48)   The Indianapolis Library was demolished to make way for a new building, and the sculpture group was put in a city storage. It was later restored and placed on a pediment in front of the new library. Dr. Hallmark addressed the dedication ceremonies on September 20, 1981.

7   (page 49)   I remember father saying he was smuggled into Deb's cell. It was my understanding that the portrait was lost in one of father's studio fires. I never knew the reason for making it.

8   (page 56)   Father made a 3½ by 2½ inch pen portrait head of himself in this costume, the only self-portrait he ever made.

9   (page 76)   Father and mother called upon him when they moved to California. Mrs. Holmes was Blanca Holmes the well-known astrolger to many film stars, and she cast horoscopes for all the family.

10 (page 79)   Father had ten studios during his career, but the two fires burned nearly all of his European sketches and drawings. He managed to save a few, but most of his early work was lost.

11 (page 83)   Mother told of a similar incident regarding a Japanese print. When she and father were married Mr. Wright gave them a print as a wedding gift. Some time later he saw it on the wall, remarked that it was "much too good," removed it and took it home with him. Mother was not amused.

12 (page 84)   Father later used plaster casts of some of these panels on the exterior of his studio in River Forest, Illinois. These plaster casts, water proofed and painted, withstood the weather for over forty years. The Larkin Building was razed in 1949 and the art works apparently lost.

13 (page 85)   In 1975 "Spring" was given to the Bock Museum in Greenville, Illinois. The whereabouts of "Winter" is unknown.

14 (page 88)   There were two splendid restaurants in the Pullman Building. One was decorated with Maxfield Parrish murals. The restaurants were operated by the Pullman Car Company, and the waiters were retired dining car waiters. The service was superb.

15 (page 90)   Mother and Mrs. Wright were active in the community. They organized a Montessori Summer School we children attended, and they supported a a Little Theater group in the small upstairs theater in the Fine Arts Building on Michigan Avenue.

Mrs. Wright was a tall, beautiful woman with a halo of redish-gold hair. An important social event one summer was a pageant held on the extensive grounds of Senator Harry Austin's estate in Oak Park, when Mrs. Wright appeared as the goddess Demeter, and Doris Humphrey, a dancing teacher who later became famous as a leading dancer in the modern dance movement, choreograpahed the pageant and appeared as Persephone. I was one of the little corphyees.

16 (page 91)   From the time I was eight until my sixteenth birthday
I was with the Wright children practically every day.
Frances was three years older than I, and Llewellyn
was three years younger. Llewellyn and my birthdays
fell on the same date, November 15, and we always
shared our birthday party.

I called Mr. Wright Uncle Frank and he called me
Dolly, I loved Mrs. Wright who was a lovely lady and
devoted to her children, but I always called her Mrs.
Wright. Mr. Wright's mother lived a few doors east
of the studio on Chicago Avenue, with her artist
daughter Maginel Wright Enright. I remember her
as an austere lady who was always called Madam
Wright by everyone.

Frances was very mischievous and was always teasing
me, or trying to manage things so I would be blamed
for them. Frances and her older sister Catherine
shared the large front bedroom in the old residence,
and there was a cot in the room where I often slept.
Frances had a pet white rat for a time and she
delighted in slipping it into my bed to frighten me.
This worked beautifully until she put it in Catherine's
bed one night, and I never saw it after that.

Mr. Wright at one time had a cage with several small,
colorful birds, and one day Frances decided it was
cruel to keep them prisoner, so she let them out the
window.

The children had a sorrel pony which seemed
enormous, and I was afraid of it. Frances insisted on
teaching me to ride it bareback, but Mrs. Wright soon
stopped that. Frances often had me in tears, but I
looked up to her and we were really good friends, and
I saw her a number of times when we both lived in
New York. The older children were too much older
to be bothered by us, except Lloyd, the oldest. He was
always saving me from Frances, and I adored him.

My sixteenth birthday was the last party Llewellyn
and I had together. I was already deeply involved with
my dancing, and for this occasion I made my own
costume and danced a solo for the guests. By this time
the Wright family was quite separated. The older
children were away at school or were involved in other
activities, and Mr. Wright was no longer there. The
following year I went to New York to pursue my
career.

17 (page 92)   After mother and father came to California, the studio was sold and was considerably modified and all of the sculpture removed.

18 (page 94)   An Australian travel folder includes this: "Lake Burley Griffin, named in his honor, is an inland sea surrounded by parklands, marinas, scenic drives and bicycle paths."

19 (page 94)   The hotel was razed in 1967.

20 (page 95)   We were all very fond of Stanley, and he gave me a fine etching of a dog's head. The studio seemed always full of people. There were always artist friends, especially the painters Leon Roecker and Alfred Juergens, C.G. Blanchard the poet, and Carl Sandburg who lived near us in a cottage on the Desplaines River in Thatcher's Woods. He loved to watch father work while they visited and he always stayed until mother invited him to lunch or dinner. Architect Robert Spencer and Isabel Roberts, and sculptor Emory Seidel, all of whom lived in River Forest, were always dropping in, Mr. Wright and of course Uncle Harry and his artist friends. There were always people passing by who just stopped in to see the studio and the garden with its pools and pieces of sculpture that were always there.

21 (page 99)   When father told Mr. Wright he would not go to Japan with him, he became very angry and accused father of "deserting" him, then said he did not need him for he had found another sculptor. This sculptor was his new mistress who was an amateur sculptress. She was unable to do the work required, and it was at this time Mr. Wright devised the technique of incorporating abstract architectural designs cast in cement in his buildings instead of sculpture. Although father and Mr. Wright never worked together again they remained lifelong friends.

22 (page 99)   The Hermes heads were actually portraits of my brother and me. The Skinners sold the house years later to friends who destroyed the fountain in a new landscaping project. Years later her daughter told me her mother was so angry at the "desecration of art" that she never spoke to them again.

23 (page 102)   Because Chicago had a very large German population it went through a special trauma during the First World War, with many inexcusable excesses. German street names were changed, and the magnificant bronze statue honoring Goethe was defaced. The most senseless and cruel reaction to the anti-German sentiment at the time was the destruction of Dachshund dogs. Our family were all dog lovers, and father in protest, made a small statue of a seated Dachshund with the word "Please" incised on the base.

24 (page 103)   Father often reworked a piece, and at one time he made a model of Nils with wings swept back in a different position. It was not nearly as effective as the original.

25 (page 107)   The Elks gave father a complimentary membership.

26 (page 123)   Father completed the group and was paid for his model, but after he left the University it was never completed in stone, and the model has been lost or destroyed.

27 (page 123)   Mr. Wright called father and told him he would come only if father said he should. Father urged him to accept.

28 (page 124)   The two old friends had a wonderful few days together. Mr. Wright was his old mischevious self and he played one more of his "jokes" on father, daring him to cut off his mustache, which fortunately soon grew back. We found Mrs. Wright a strong and gracious woman, and I enjoyed talking with her for she had been a dancer when she was young.

29 (page 125)   Dean Lawrence was unstinting in his praise of father and what he had accomplished in building his department. Father taught three full years including summer sessions, and he was a year over retirement age. He had often had students in his own studio and he taught classes in sculpture at both Loyola Seminary and the Lutheran College in River Forest. His teaching methods, which were very effective, were unorthodox. The students were enthusiastic about his classes and he thoroughly enjoyed teaching.

30 (page 125)   It has often been asked why father made so few of his studio works in permanent materials. The reason was that he loved to experiment with an idea, to rethink and enlarge upon the original. He had no false pride in an original work, but would rework a model many times, sometimes putting it aside for months and even years. Most of the works in his collection are in plaster for they were made for a touring exhibit, later to be cast in bronze.

31 (page 126)   Many furnaces burned sawdust which was purchased at the nearby saw mill. It made wonderful fuel for it burned with an intense heat and caked into a hot mass which burned for hours. We were fascinated by the kitchen stove in the house we rented, which was half wood-burning and half electric. Wood was everywhere and cheap, and so was electricity because of the abundant water power.

32 (page 130)   Both of these manuscripts, photos and plates are in the Bock Musuem at Greenville College in Greenville, Illinois.

33 (page 133)   Mother and father had made many friends among the faculty during their stay in Eugene. Mother had been active in the Faculty Women's Club, and we all enjoyed the campus atmosphere and were socially active until we left.

34 (page 133)   It was a habit of our family to have a glass of wine with dinner. In Eugene mother experimented with making cherry wine from the abundance of cherries from a tree in our yard. When we were making plans to leave Thor got a small wine barrel, filled it with mother's wine and packed it in the back of the car. As we rode along it would occasionally give out a noticable gurgle, and as Prohibition had just recently been repealed we became concerned as we approached the California Border Agricultural Station. They passed us without comment, and we teased mother for a long time about being a bootlegger.

#

35 (page 143)   Father also patented an ice hoist at the time when refrigeration was by heavy blocks of ice. This hoist could lift huge blocks of ice to the second story of a building. His brother manufactured and sold them for a time.

36 (page 145)   A set of the children's pottery dishes, and the salt and pepper shakers are in the collection of the Richard W. Bock Museum at Greenville College, Greenville, Illinois.